PLAY SNOOKER

with DENNIS TAYLOR

PLAY SNOOKER
with DENNIS TAYLOR

Written in collaboration with Clive Everton

Edited by Gordon Menzies

BBC BOOKS

Published by BBC Books,
a division of BBC Enterprises Limited,
Woodlands, 80 Wood Lane, London W12 0TT

First published 1990
© Dennis Taylor, Clive Everton and Gordon Menzies 1990

ISBN 0 563 36037 2

Set in Helvetica by Butler & Tanner Ltd, Frome, Somerset
Printed and bound in Great Britain by Butler & Tanner Ltd, Frome, Somerset
Colour printing by Lawrence Allen Ltd, Weston-super-Mare
Cover printed in England by Richard Clay Ltd, St Ives Plc

CONTENTS

ACKNOWLEDGEMENTS

The author would like to thank Clive Everton and Philip Yates for their help in compiling this book.

FOREWORD

One of the main reasons for snooker's comfortable modern image has been the play and demeanour of players like Dennis Taylor.

Some people claim that the fun has gone out of snooker and at top level it is a serious business, but Dennis Taylor, a real character and a true gentleman, reminds everybody that enjoyment is a vital part of the game, for players and spectators alike. Dennis and I have had some epic battles, though none so great as the World Championship final in 1985 when Dennis beat me on the black of the 35th and final frame. This was painful for me but a famous win for him, and the warmth of the public's reception of it is a reflection of his popularity.

Snooker is a complex game. In this book – rather like his style of playing – Dennis tries to keep his instruction simple. If you are an experienced player, you will get some useful hints on how to improve your game. If you are thinking of taking up the game for the first time, Dennis gives excellent advice on how to get started. But whether you are a beginner or a club regular, you are bound to gain from the sensible, straightforward approach that Dennis recommends.

Snooker is also a fun game, to be enjoyed by all the family. Read on, enjoy yourselves. Play snooker with Dennis Taylor.

1 START THE RIGHT WAY

THE GAME OF SNOOKER

While millions of people regularly watch hours of snooker on
television, many still do not fully understand how the game is
played or the rules that govern it.

Snooker is played on a standard billiard table. It has a level bed
of two-inch-thick slate. Its cushions are made of rubber and its
cloth surface is of blended wools. Full size tables, the ones used
for all professional and amateur tournaments, measure 11 feet $8\frac{1}{2}$
inches by 5 feet 10 inches, inside the cushion faces.

At the start of every frame (the name given to a single game)
there are fifteen reds, six colours and a white (the cue-ball) on
the table. The balls carry points value. The reds are each worth
one point, the yellow is worth two, the green three, brown four,
blue five, pink six and black, the highest value ball on the table,
seven points.

A frame is won by scoring more points than your opponent,
both by potting the balls into the table's six pockets, and by
gaining penalty points from any foul stroke committed by your
opponent. Matches are made up of an agreed number of frames.
The common length of amateur matches is the best of three, five
or seven frames, while the final of the World Professional
Championship is contested over 35 frames.

A player's initial objective is to pot a red. If they succeed, they
must then play one of the six colours. If they pot a colour it is
replaced and the player then plays another red. This process
continues until all fifteen reds have disappeared and only the six
colours remain. The colours must then be potted in ascending
numerical order, ie yellow first, and black last. When a player fails
to pot the ball 'on', then it is his or her opponent's turn at the table.

When the black has been potted or a foul committed it is the
end of the frame, unless the scores are tied. In this case the black
is re-spotted.

THE BREAK

To start a frame, the first player places the cue-ball anywhere in
the 'D' and then hits it into the pyramid of reds. This is called the
break, or break-off shot. Contact must be made with at least one

red. If, with the break-off, you miscue, fail to reach the reds or hit one of the colours first, it is a foul shot.

STRIKING THE BALL

The only ball the cue may make contact with is the white. It must be struck cleanly with the cue tip. For a stroke to be deemed fair all the balls must be at rest. No balls may be forced off the playing surface of the table. The player must be touching the ground with at least one foot, and the cue-ball must be hit only once.

FOUL SHOTS

The minimum penalty for a foul stroke is four points, but if you foul the blue, pink or black you lose five, six or seven points respectively. The most common foul shots arise from pocketing the white (known as an in-off), failure to hit the 'object-ball' (ie the ball 'on'), or from hitting the wrong ball (for example the blue when aiming at a red). Other less common foul shots are touching a ball with your clothing or hands, playing a shot with both feet off the ground and striking the cue-ball while other balls are still moving.

There are a number of other basic rules with which it pays to be acquainted, and a lack of knowledge in this department has been the downfall of many an inexperienced player. See page 111 for a list of basic rules.

THE SNOOKER

Most fouls are committed because of accidental errors. But with a weapon known as the 'snooker' it is possible to entrap your opponent and make them struggle to make contact with the object-ball. Laying snookers is one of the most skilful aspects of the game. A typical example occurs when a player is supposed to hit a red but their direct path is blocked by intervening colours. In such a situation contact with the ball 'on' can only be made by swerving the white or by playing it off one or more cushions. In such a case the risk of missing the object-ball is obviously much greater than if a direct strike were possible.

FREE BALL

If you find yourself snookered after your opponent has committed a foul shot a provision in the rules allows you to play for any colour you nominate, ie a free ball. If the reds are obscured but, for example, the blue is hanging over a pocket, it can be nominated and will be treated like a normal red and count as one point if potted. It will, however, be replaced on its spot after it has been potted. In such circumstances the blue would count as only one point and not its normal five point value.

There is one very important point to remember about free balls. It is a foul shot (and a free ball to your opponent) if you leave them snookered behind the particular colour you have nominated as a free ball. The only exception to this rule is when only the pink and black remain on the table.

PUSH STROKE

Push strokes are not permissible. They occur when the cue-tip, cue-ball and object-ball are in simultaneous contact. A knowledgeable referee can detect a push stroke by the way the various balls react, and also by the sound the shot makes. Push strokes usually happen when the cue and object balls are very close together.

TOUCHING BALL

Sometimes the white comes to rest against another ball. In this case the next player must play the cue-ball away without causing even the slightest movement in the ball it was touching. If the touching ball moves, it is deemed a push stroke.

PLAY AGAIN RULE

After any foul shot a player who finds himself in an awkward position has the right to ask his opponent to play again. This helps the player who does not have a 'free ball' and so does not fancy the next shot, usually because the path back to safety is strewn with obstacles.

PROBLEMS WITH SPOTTING COLOURS

Occasionally when a particular colour has been potted, it cannot be replaced on its spot because the spot is occupied by another ball. In this instance the colour is placed on the highest value spot that is available. Sometimes, all six spots are covered, in which case the colour is placed as near as possible to its own spot in a direct line with the top (black) cushion. Knowing exactly where colour balls will be positioned after they have been potted can be crucial to breakbuilding. However, you must judge by eye alone whether a colour can be replaced on its spot or not. You cannot ask the referee to check, and it is a foul if you use a ball from a pocket to check it yourself.

THE JUMP SHOT

Jumping the white over an intervening ball is a foul, but no foul is committed if the cue-ball jumps into the air after it has contacted the object-ball.

SELECTING A CUE

Perhaps the most important decision one has to make when starting to play snooker is selecting a suitable cue. People who do not play regularly often use communal cues from the rack at their club or snooker centre, but anyone with serious intentions to improve must purchase their own. It is a worthwhile investment for any player because as one gets used to the idiosyncracies of the cue, confidence and consistency increase. It also allows the player to ensure the good treatment of his or her cue.

The rules require the cue to be at least three feet long. It is usual to select one which reaches about $2\frac{1}{2}$ inches below shoulder level, and weighing anything between 16 and 18 ounces. These are only guidelines, however. The optimum length and weight of a cue is, in the final analysis, down to the player using it. Joe Bloggs may feel a particular cue is perfection while Joe Soap may think the same one is best used as firewood.

Many players now have two-piece cues. They are now made to a high standard and of course they are easily transportable

If you go into a sports shop to purchase a cue, make sure they allow you to try it out before you buy it. If it doesn't suit your requirements you will be able to change it and try out another one. This may be impractical, but if your local club sells cues they will almost certainly let you experiment with it. It doesn't matter a jot how expensive or cheap the cue is. It's all a matter of trial and error and personal preference.

The best cues are made from maple or ash. The one-piece cue remained standard until about fifteen years ago, but two-piece cues, with either a wood or a stainless steel joint, have come very much into favour in the last few years. Steve Davis and Jimmy White use these type of cues, and so do I. I've got a two-piece ash cue, with the join three-quarters of the way down towards the butt. It is important when choosing an ash cue to make sure that the grain is running the right way, from butt to tip.

I used a one-piece cue for many years but, as with so many other players, I changed because of the inconvenience of carrying the long cue around with me. I remember well humping it around in my early amateur days when I was involved in league matches. I had this great cumbersome case and while sitting at the back of the bus I had to hold it in the air. If someone got on and the bus set off unexpectedly the first thing they used to grab for was my cue case. It was very embarrassing.

If you buy a cue and begin to feel that it is not the one for you, do not think that you have to stick with it. Obviously chopping and changing willy-nilly can be damaging, but persevering with an unsuitable cue will not promote the confidence that every player needs. Some top players, like Ray Reardon and Alex Higgins, have had major problems when their trusty cues were stolen or broken, and found it difficult to adapt to new ones. Luckily I've been able to adjust, and in the past few months I think I've stumbled across a cue that will serve me well in the future. I was at my old friend Ian Woosnam's house for the weekend, and when we walked into his purpose-built snooker room for a session I realised that I had forgotten my cue. Forced to look through the rack I found a reasonable looking implement with which I immediately made two century breaks. I felt I'd been using it for years. I asked Ian if I could borrow it, and I've been playing with it ever since.

Always treat your cue with respect. Maintained properly it will serve you well for a long time. The occasional wipe with a damp cloth will help to keep it clean and prevent the cue from becoming sticky and uncomfortable to play with. It is also worth remembering that extremes of temperature can warp the cue. Therefore, do not leave it in the car overnight or in the kitchen. Finally, keep it safe; should you lose your cue through theft your form will most likely suffer.

Many two-piece cues allow an extension to be fitted which means that a player can use his or her own tip for virtually every shot

THE TIP

Once the cue has been selected, make sure that its tip is up to standard. The best tips are Elk Master or Blue Diamond. A hard tip is preferable to a spongy, soft one which makes it difficult to assess the strength needed for a shot. However, if the tip is too hard the cue-ball will tend to skid off and become difficult to control. Tip shape is also vital. When one buys a cue it usually comes complete with an unused, unshaped tip that is flat and, most likely, hard. To give maximum responsiveness on shots, the tip should be gently domed. This shape is easily achieved either with a special plastic container which has sandpaper in it, a file, or just an ordinary lump of sandpaper. In the past players have even used the rough, sulphur-based side of a box of matches. But, whatever you use, the secret is to dome the tip with one-way strokes so that the tip fibres are not ruined. Eventually, after five or ten minutes of intensive work, a nicely domed tip will appear.

THE CHALK

The 'perfect' cue and the most responsive of tips would be rendered useless without the constant use of the smallest, but essential, piece of a player's equipment: a block of chalk. Without this, you will miscue constantly. Before almost every stroke you will notice that professionals and top amateurs take the chalk out of their pocket and apply it gently to the tip. Perhaps this constant chalking is not always needed, but it is better to be safe than sorry.

Most knowledgeable players use either Triangle or National Tournament chalk, both of which are manufactured in the USA. At the moment I'm using LEP chalk which is made in England and will hopefully prove to be as good as the American stuff.

Green chalk is definitely the best colour because it tends not to stick to the cue-ball. Blue is also all right but try to avoid the gimmicky red chalk. This can ruin the cloth as it leaves unsightly marks. And some clubs, realising the damage that it can cause, have banned it.

RESTS AND EXTENSIONS

All tables have accessories known as rests. The purpose of a rest is to help players reach a particular shot which, without assistance, they could not possibly attempt. Normally, they are approximately 5 feet long with an 'X'-shaped head, usually fashioned out of steel or plastic. The purpose of the rest-heads is to hold the cue firmly in position while a shot is being played. It thus replaces the player's bridge hand. In my experience the plastic variety should be avoided whenever possible. They are so light that stability is not guaranteed when a power shot is being played. As we have said, rests belong to the table not the player. One exception to this is the Bedford professional Nigel Gilbert, who wears a white silk glove on his bridge hand and who carries his

Only constant chalking of the cue after almost every shot will help a player to reduce the risk of miscue to the maximum. I find that green chalk is best

*The three legs of the tripod.
Rigid back leg, bent left leg,
and straight bridge arm*

own rest, with a slightly smaller head than usual, from tournament to tournament.

Implements known as the spider, the half-butt and the three quarter-butt are also available for use when the balls finish in a really awkward position. The spider, of which there are now many different types, is designed to allow cueing over intervening balls by supplying an artificially high bridge. If there is more than one ball getting in the way you may be required to hunt out the extended spider.

If the white is a long way out of reach down the table, the length of the normal rest may be inadequate. In such a situation the half-butt or the three quarter-butt is needed.

Without doubt the three quarter-butt is the most difficult rest to use for a number of reasons. Its length and its instability are the obvious ones, but its oversize and undershaped tip (remember it's not in continual use) make certain advanced positional shots virtually impossible for even the best of players.

These 'monsters' have been a blight on everyone's life for years until now when they are slowly being made obsolete by a wonderful, yet simple, invention known as the cue extension. Most professionals carry them around now and they have become as much part of the equipment as the rests themselves. Made to a variety of lengths they slip on the end of the cue and/or the rest to give a player vital extra reach. Their advantage is that one's own cue-tip can now be used for virtually every shot.

THE STANCE

In common with every sport the most important things in snooker are the basics. It is crucial to start off correctly, otherwise it is almost certain that you will develop more and more bad habits as you go along. The three basics of snooker are a player's stance, their grip of the cue and the way they form their bridge.

The stance of a boxer or a marksman is quite similar to that of a snooker player. Above all, be comfortable. Do not compromise what you feel happy with just to become a carbon copy of your hero, who may have a totally different physical make-up. Basically you should be in a position where, if someone came up behind you and gave you a little shove you would still be able to retain your balance.

Your front leg (the left if you are right-handed) should be bent, with the foot pointing in the direction of the intended shot. At the same time your back leg should be as straight as is comfortably possible to ensure that maximum stability is attained. Be careful not to let your chest become too square on the shot.

I am even-sighted so my cue runs under the middle of my chin and my weight is more on my left leg than my right. However, players who are pronounced right-eye sighters will tend to have their weight slightly more on their right leg.

20

A pronounced left-eye sighter will tend to have a very sideways-on stance, with his right foot pointing out almost at right angles. An even-sighted player like myself will not be quite so sideways-to the shot and their right foot will be at roughly 45 degrees. Right-eye sighters tend to stand quite square to the shot.

The relative position of your feet is important. Do not have them almost touching each other or, conversely, too far apart. Like most aspects of the game, finding the best stance for you requires experimentation. Tinkering with a car often leads to it being finely tuned and a similar principle applies here. The distance between your feet is largely dependent upon your height. A 6 foot 4 inch giant, like Australian World Cup player John Campbell, has a much wider stance than Tony Meo for example.

Ideally, the stance adopted should allow the cue to run as horizontally as possible. The cue should also brush lightly against your chest as this acts as an aid to straight-cueing, the most important factor in accurate snooker. Straight-cueing not only breeds accuracy but also consistency which is the hallmark of class.

BRIDGE

While the grips and stances of most professionals have minor idiosyncrasies the bridge does not differ much from player to player. Think of the bridge as the front leg of a tripod, the rear

The bridge hand should be raised in a slight hump, the fingers should grip the cloth and the thumb should be cocked to form a channel between it and the forefinger

parts of which are your own legs. The bridge's importance to a player's overall game cannot be understated and many people ruin their chances of improvement by sticking with a bridge that, for one reason or another, is ineffective.

The making of an effective bridge is simplicity itself. Place your hand on the table (the left if you are right-handed), spread your fingers apart, pull from knuckles up while gripping the cloth with your finger pads and then raise or cock your thumb – you have the perfect bridge hand.

By pulling the finger pads inwards, the hand becomes raised in a slight hump. Consequently the hand is now resting on the underpart of the thumb, the fingertips and its heel. By cocking the thumb high a channel will be formed between the fingers and thumb. This will allow the cue to travel through when the shot is being played. Be careful, though, if this channel is too wide you will find it impossible to stop the cue wobbling from side to side as you make your shot. As straightness of cueing should be your primary concern at all times, this is a considerable disadvantage.

By gripping the cloth with the finger pads and by thrusting out the cue-arm as straight as possible, the bridge hand will remain solid. This solidity makes it easier for a player to line up or target a particular shot while it also reduces the dreaded body movement. Sometimes a player grips the cloth so fiercely that their fingermarks can be seen on the table long after the shot has been played. In the 1930s Fred Davis, a former World Champion and brother of the legendary Joe Davis, was heavily criticised for marking tables with the pressure of his fingertips. The bridge could not have been a bad one though, because Fred only lost the world title once between 1948 and 1956.

Conversely, by raising your hand too high, keeping the cue as horizontal as possible to the cue-ball will be made extremely difficult. Some players are forever hitting down on the white, and as I will explain more fully later on, this causes sidespin to be imparted, so the cue-ball will swerve and deviate from its intended course.

Most players have the bridge hand between 7 and 8 inches from the cue-ball. Tall people need to bend their bridge arm more than the average size player to avoid 'standing off' the cue-ball and making a correct follow-through physically impossible.

THE GRIP

When you are reasonably happy with your stance and bridge you need to turn your attention to a sound grip. The idea of this varies from player to player. Differences stem from where they hold the cue in relation to the butt, how many fingers they have on the cue at any one time and, leading on from that, how loosely or fiercely they grip the cue.

With this last dilemma a compromise grip needs to be found. It

At the moment I grip the cue about two inches from the end

is vital that you don't grip the cue too tightly, because then, if you are under any kind of pressure, it is quite likely that you will snatch at the shot. Conversely, if you hold the cue lightly with just the tips of the fingers, as the majority of nineteenth and early twentieth-century billiards players did, certain shots which are an integral part of modern snooker and involve powerful striking, like stun and screw, will pose bigger problems than they should. Basically, your hold on the cue should be just firm enough to keep it under control. Never allow your wrist to become floppy. The stroke should be carried through with cue, hand, wrist and forearm all working in harmony.

Having said that I remember that when I won the 1985 World Championship I was holding my cue very loosely. In fact the cue was resting on my fingers while my thumb wasn't doing anything. It might not have been textbook but who cares? I felt extremely comfortable and confident with it. Like so many aspects of this game, what works for one may not work for another. Only by experimentation can a player decide what grip is best for them.

Physical characteristics also mean that it would be entirely wrong to propound the notion of a uniform grip that would produce equally beneficial results for all. This can be seen down at the local snooker centre every day of the week. If, for example,

On the backswing it is technically advisable to release the grip of the back two fingers, letting the first two do the work

(Right) A back view of my grip, showing a 'tender' unfierce hold on the cue

your wrist tends to turn to the right, like me, the grip tends to go more towards the fingers. Conversely if the wrist is naturally inclined to turn your hand to the left, thus causing your elbow to jut out from your body, the cue will, most likely, be held in the palm. This was the kind of grip that took Ray Reardon to six world titles in the 1970s. After sustaining a broken shoulder in a boyhood accident Ray's elbow jutted violently out from his body. This is unorthodox, but what does this matter if it suits him?

The question remains as to how we avoid the potentially damaging fierce grip, while retaining enough control to play power, stun and screw, shots? The answer is simple. The grip of the second and third fingers can be eased ever so slightly on the backswing, and as the cue is pushed towards the cue-ball the grip of these fingers should be re-applied. Throughout this process it is important that the strength of grip of first finger and thumb should remain constant.

As for the little finger, this can be taken away from the cue altogether, but should always be relaxed. The strength of the little finger is insignificant in what, to all intents and purposes, is a three-finger flexible grip. Steve Davis, Jimmy White and John Parrott are all able to produce gasps from the crowd after seemingly effortless deep screw shots or the like, because they employ this 'best of both worlds' approach to gripping their cues.

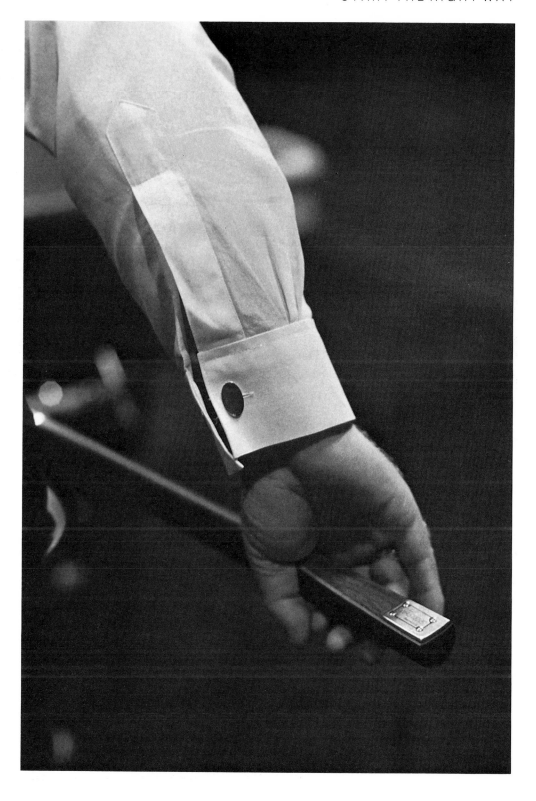

2 LEARNING TO POT

Potting. That's what all snooker players love to do. Nothing gives more satisfaction than a long pot the whole length of the table, particularly if the cue-ball comes back into a good position for the next shot. The sound of the intended ball going into the intended pocket is music to the ears. Inch perfect positioning is also a sight for sore eyes but it is important that we don't move too quickly. Obtaining a good cue-ball position can come later, and in this chapter we will just concentrate on the theory and the art of potting.

CHECKING THE BASICS

Before you attempt to strike the cue-ball, re-check the basics. Remember the boxer and the marksman. Always try to make yourself feel comfortable with the stance. Feet should not be too close or far apart, but at the optimum distance where they allow the stance to fulfil its primary function – stability – on the shot.

The third leg of the 'tripod' is the bridge. Remember, the hand should be between 6 and 8 inches away from the cue-ball with the knuckles raised, with the thumb nicely cocked and the finger pads clutching on to the cloth. Finally, check the grip. Is it too loose or too fierce? Make doubly sure your grip has enough firmness to stop the wrist of your cue-arm becoming floppy. As with the stance, the most effective type of grip is the one with which the individual feels most comfortable.

SIGHTING

A player can posses the most straight and unerring cue-action in the history of the game, but if their alignment is incorrect they will quickly find that potting can be a frustration, with balls 'inexplicably' missing their intended targets at regular intervals. As snooker is rightly recognised as a game with a small margin of error, the importance of correct sighting is obviously enormous.

For years the orthodox advice for sighting was to ensure that the cue would lightly brush the chin directly below the nose, in order that both eyes could concentrate on the pot. However, this advice assumes that the player has eyes of equal strength. While this may be the case in a large number of cases some players

Long pots are difficult and require accurate sighting, straight cue delivery and plenty of practice

*(Left) Everything in line-
practise up and down the
colour spots.*

have one eye, the 'master eye', stronger than the other. Joe Davis's master eye was his left, while of the modern day professionals John Virgo and Steve Newbury are the most pronounced right-eyed sighters.

This is all very well, I hear you say, but how do we find out which is our master eye? The answer is simple. Place a piece of chalk at the baulk end of the table, and stand directly in front of it at the other end. Then point your finger at the chalk while keeping both eyes open. Close your right eye and see if your finger is still pointing at the chalk. If you find it is, you are left-eyed. This is easily confirmed, because if you close your left eye you will have to move your finger in order for it to remain pointing at the chalk. The revelation of discovering which eye, if either, is the master eye will have a major influence on your snooker fortunes, because if the eye which is doing the sighting is not directly over the cue there will be a strong tendency to strike across the ball causing unwanted side to be imparted on to the cue-ball.

*Note how the elbow, head
and cue run in a straight line
through to the cue-ball*

The next problem with sighting is to determine where you should be looking at the precise moment you strike the cue-ball. There are basic rules for this that all coaches worth their salt will drum into their pupils.

At the moment of impact between cue-tip and white the player *must* be fixing his gaze at the point on the object-ball where contact is needed for the attempted pot to be successful. Using an analogy with another sport clarifies this further. If Seve Ballesteros looked at the hole the moment he struck the golf ball, instead of watching the putter head as it made contact with the ball, the chances are that even with his genius the putt would go astray.

This is similar to the two major sighting faults in snooker, which can lead to even the most straightforward of pots being missed. How many times have you seen someone at your local club line up a blue into the middle pocket perfectly correctly only, at the last fraction of a second, to switch his eyes from the blue to the pack of reds that he is trying to break up. The blue is consequently missed because the eyes have been in the wrong place at the wrong time. And how many people look at the pocket at the wrong moment in a premature attempt to discover if the ball has gone in, and miss the shot as a result?

We all appreciate that the positioning of the cue-ball is important, but always remember that your eyes are only a potting aid. Where you strike the cue-ball and the relative strength of the shot will determine where the cue-ball finishes, nothing else. Never forget the rule – keep your eyes on the object-ball when the cue-ball is being struck.

CUE-ACTION

If your sighting, and therefore your alignment, are spot on, a straight, effective cue-action will make you a very good exponent of the game. It would not be too much to say that without doubt the cue-action is the single most important ally for a good player.

Before hitting the cue-ball it is advisable to make a number of preliminary strokes. These should be short, rhythmic and smooth but do not make contact. This 'feathering' when addressing the ball is useful to steady and settle a player for the shot ahead. It is snooker's equivalent of a golfer's waggles, or the movement of a cricketer's bat in the crease as the bowler runs in. Like the majority of professionals I usually take four or five preliminary strokes, but it all depends upon your attitude and personality. Some players, like Tony Knowles for example, make a large number of preliminary waggles while others, like Cliff Thorburn, only feather the cue once or twice.

When actually playing the shot imagine that your elbow is a hinge which will open and close during the cue-action. As the cue is drawn back the hinge opens. Then it is gradually closed as the cue goes through the white and on into the follow-through. Always remember that the straightness of the cue-action is vital, and so the importance of preventing the hinge twisting during the stroke is obvious.

Remember that the movement of the cue-arm, mainly from elbow to wrist, should be the one and only force that drives the cue through the ball. Any movement of the shoulders and upper body will lead to the head coming up. And as we have seen, any head and consequently eye-movement on the shot can lead to failure. If stillness is compromised so is accuracy. Stephen Hendry keeps his head very, very still.

Novices, possibly over-eager to find out if they have successfully potted a ball, will often raise their heads to look before the stroke has been completed with disastrous results. This is obviously a basic fault but one which, by no stretch of the imagination, is confined to beginners. Even the most advanced players, myself included, have been known to throw our heads in the air, especially after a shot that requires a lot of power.

Just take a close look next time you watch Steve Davis on television. You will soon begin to notice that on virtually every shot his upper body and head remain down and in position long after the cue-ball has been despatched. This is a legacy of the intensive, theory-based, practice sessions he and father Bill went through in the early days. Bill would stand with a cue just a fraction above his son's head when Steve was playing a forcing shot. If Steve's head came up slightly it hit the cue and the shot would be replayed until the movement was eradicated. This often went on for hours, and now Steve's head never moves. When he plays a shot he just concentrates on the basics – keeping still and delivering the cue in a straight line.

Faults also rear their heads, for want of a better phrase, during the backswing. Ideally, the cue should be taken back smoothly, should pause for a fraction of a second then begin its forward path towards the cue-ball. Some players draw the cue back with disjointed jerky movements while others, particularly for power shots, draw it back much too far, well above the horizontal. The stroke should end, as it began, with the cue directly in line with the shot. The cue should go through the cue-ball for several inches, before stopping along the same line. If this piston-like cue-action is achieved you will have realised your objective – to make the cue-ball, and consequently the object-ball, go precisely where they are aimed.

Even if your cue-action seems to be functioning adequately, never be afraid to make minor adjustments; there is always room for improvement. Terry Griffiths, who won the World Championship at his first attempt in 1979 – beating me in the final – is one of snooker's great 'tinkers', always looking to improve his technique.

When starting to play snooker it is important to understand that

(Overleaf) This close-up sequence displays the ideal distance the bridge hand should be from the cue-ball at address (top left), and also illustrates the optimum backswing and follow-through required for a 'normal' shot.
Some novices take the cue back much too far. There is no need for a longer backswing than this (bottom left).
Push the cue through the ball in a straight line (top right). Make sure you follow through after the cue has made contact with the white (bottom right). Don't snatch

If you place two reds either side of the pink spot and the cue-ball returns over the spot without touching, then your cue delivery is straight

it is almost impossible to become a carbon copy of your favourite player. By all means pick out the things that are right about their cue-action or their stance, but never forget that in the end it is up to you to develop your own style, approach and method.

EXERCISES TO TEST STRAIGHTNESS OF CUEING
There are two widely used practice exercises designed with the purpose of showing a player that his cue-action is straight, or more likely, where he is going wrong.

The first of these could not be simpler but over the years even the greatest players have used it. Place the cue-ball on the brown spot then hit it over the blue, pink and black spots. If, on the return journey from the top cushion, the cue-ball does not come back over the spots but veers to either the left or right a problem has

been diagnosed. Knocking the cue-ball up and down the spots may seem the easiest thing imaginable for the uninitiated. This opinion quickly changes after the first few attempts.

If the ball strays away from the spots on coming back up the table the player has imparted some unintentional sidespin on to the cue-ball. This can be caused by a whole variety of things, poor alignment, problems with stance or a defective bridge. To solve the problem continue to persevere with your cue-action and sighting until the sidespin has disappeared, allowing the white to follow a straight course. Fred Davis practised this shot for hours on end during his heyday, and Steve Davis, generally recognised as the possessor of one of the truest cue-actions in the modern game, often begins his solo practice sessions by playing this shot for half an hour or so.

To make this exercise more interesting place two reds beyond the black spot, near the top cushion, with just enough room between them for the cue-ball to get through. If the cue-ball hits one of the reds you are cueing incorrectly. Practise till you're better.

Frank Callan, one of the best-known snooker coaches in the country, agrees that while regular practice at striking the cue-ball properly is essential for all players who want to maintain a high standard, this shot over the brown, blue, pink and black spots can sometimes be misleading. This is because a player can impart a smidgen of side on to the cue-ball which will correct itself on the far cushion even if it is slightly off-line on the outward journey from the cue. If you are worried check this by placing a small chalk mark at the point on the cushion where the white is supposed to hit. However, as a result Frank has developed an exercise which doesn't even require a cue-ball! He quite rightly states that a player can discover whether (or not) they are cueing straight by aiming at an imaginary white along the baulk line. The cue should be obscuring the baulk line from the player's view throughout the stroke. Basically if the cue goes off-line the player would be hitting across the cue-ball. With this problem it is possible to impart side even if the cue-ball is struck in the right place.

This exercise also highlights any defects with the bridge. If, once the stroke has been completed, the cue drifts to the right (for the right-hander) it is a symptom of the thumb on the bridge hand being too low. If it drifts to the left, you've guessed it, the thumb is too high.

While this exercise may sound the ultimate in boring practice chores its rewards are high. What you must realise is that potting has its foundation in correct alignment and straightness of cue-action. Their importance to any player cannot be overstated.

THEORY OF POTTING

Consistent, accurate potting is a prerequisite for successful snooker. Until a player can pot well enough to string together sizeable breaks his armoury is not well enough stocked with ammunition to win the battle. A professional player will take less out of himself killing off a frame with one break than winning it in bits and pieces.

When taking the first steps in snooker it is often tempting to try to hasten your skill development by attempting advanced positional shots whenever possible. This is a dangerous approach – don't run before you can walk.

A pot is completed by the cue-ball striking the object-ball in such a way that it is propelled into the pocket. One thing is sure though. While the abstract theory of potting can be explained in these simple terms, putting the theory into practice can be most infuriating and bewildering.

If you have a straight pot, one where the pocket, cue-ball and object-ball are in a straight line, a full-ball contact between cue and object-ball is needed. Fortunately, for the sake of avoiding boring repetition the vast majority of pots are not straight and therefore require the object-ball to be sent off at an angle.

Sometimes, half, quarter or three-quarter ball contacts are needed. When a half-ball contact is required the cue-ball must cover exactly half the surface of the object-ball at the precise moment of impact. If the white strikes the object-ball so that it covers more than half it is said to have been struck too full. The object-ball will be 'undercut' and will miss the pocket. Conversely if the white catches the object less than half ball – too thinly – it is said to have been 'overcut' and will again miss the pocket, but this time on the opposite side.

While they may seem straightforward enough on paper, the subleties of potting are so many and so varied that it is almost impossible to know how to pot well without any experience on a snooker table itself. You can have the best cue-action around and unerring alignment, yet if you do not know where to hit the balls in order to pot them these are useless. Lack of knowledge leads to novices missing easy pots. However, as time goes on and a player's experience increases, these elementary mistakes should crop up less regularly. In snooker, as in most other games, it is vitally important to learn from your errors. If you play as often as you possibly can, pots that once posed a major problem will gradually become second nature. The type of contact required is learnt from experience. At the start it is all too easy to become exasperated, but it is important to be persistent, things will get better.

If, after considerable practice, you are still struggling to get the balls into the pockets – because you cannot get the angles right – just try to imagine that there is a third ball resting on the near side

This is a three-quarter ball pot

Here a half-ball pot is required. If the object-ball is struck too thickly it will veer to the right of the pocket (as we look at it)

of the object-ball in a direct line away from the centre of the intended pocket. If you then retain the position of this imaginary ball in your memory, and aim the cue-ball exactly at the point on the object-ball where it was touching (ie full on the imaginary ball), your success rate will increase. It may also help to remember that the contact point for a pot is always on the point of the object-ball furthest from the pocket.

Everyone from Steve Davis to the most humble club player goes through this learning process. There is absolutely no substitute for practice. It is an important facet of the game. Never let your head drop if you miss a simple opportunity. Everyone blunders at one time or another. The key is to reduce your mistakes to a minimum. If you are consistent with the easy ones, you will start to pot a few hard ones.

PRACTISE YOUR POTTING

We have seen earlier in this chapter how best to practise and develop the straightness of your cue-action. But how do you get the most out of potting practice?

(Right) A fine cut, which involves clipping the object-ball at less than quarter-ball, is required here

The first exercise is beneficial for players at all levels. Attempt some straight pots with six reds placed quite close together across the table, and approximately 12 inches from the baulk line and

A straight pot requires the white and object-ball to make a full-ball contact

parallel to it. Now place the white on the baulk line, make each pot dead straight and attempt to pot each red into the furthest pocket. If you are successful with each pot then it is obvious that you are cueing correctly. If you miss, as at some stage you undoubtedly will, stay down on the shot. Look to see if the cue is aiming at the middle of the intended pocket at the end of the follow-through. If it has deviated from the pocket you can confidently say that you are not cueing as straight as you should.

Continue to practise that type of shot. If you are successful try moving the reds further away from the baulk line until they are directly between the two middle pockets. The cue-ball now has further to travel before making contact with the reds. It is therefore logical that the margin of error increases as the distance between cue-ball and object-ball increases. Steve Davis once placed all 21 balls along the centre of the table (15 reds and the six colours) and potted the first 19. That's his record for this exercise. Keep trying to set a personal record for yourself. This is the perfect routine for promoting straight-cueing.

So after all that advice, how do you become a better potter? It all comes down to accurate aiming, straight-cueing and practice. For a novice even playing on a small table or playing a game of pool in your local pub will help, especially in becoming accustomed to all the different angles. If you miss don't get downhearted. No one is infallible. If your cueing action is sound and your eyesight is good you won't go far wrong. If your eyesight isn't what it might be a visit to the optician is obviously worthwhile. Glasses certainly worked wonders for me, but that's another story.

3 CONTROLLING THE CUE-BALL

If you want to become a good snooker player and be able to make frame clinching breaks consistently, it is imperative that you learn how to control the cue-ball. You can be the most dangerous potter in your club but if the cue-ball constantly runs out of position you'll end up losing an awful lot of games. However, if you are aware how the cue-ball is going to react after a pot, and you can control that reaction for your own benefit, you are well on the way to becoming a winner.

Obviously, complete beginners are just content to pot the balls, but good snooker hinges on players' positional skills either for leaving themselves easy shots or, as is often overlooked, leaving opponents in awkward positions. This chapter is an explanation of the positional shots required to build big breaks. There is no great mystery to unravel with breakbuilding. Breaks are compiled with a combination of shots. It is possible, with a heaven-sent set-up of the balls, to run in a reasonable break with a series of plain-ball shots. But these gilt-edged opportunities are rare.

Perrie Mans, the South African who reached the final of the 1978 World Championship, was a brilliant potter in his heyday, but when the edge went off his potting his lack of cue-ball control virtually finished him as a professional.

WHAT ARE THE PROBLEMS WITH POSITIONAL PLAY?
The difficulty with positional play is that it splits your attention, because you have to attempt to control the object-ball and the cue-ball simultaneously. For the novice this two-ball control can be very demanding because they need all their concentration just to pot the ball. Of course advanced players play the range of positional shots almost as second nature.

But I'm sure that everyone who has played the game will have missed a relatively easy pot because their concentration was too heavily focused on the positional aspect of the other balls. Just listen closely to the comments at your club. 'I was thinking too hard about getting on the black' or 'Why didn't I just pot it' are two of the most common remarks heard after a player has failed to pot a ball because they're worrying about cue-ball control. However, in making these statements, the key, as in learning about potting itself, is that you must learn from your mistakes.

For this particular shot (i.e. a left to right swerve) you need to strike the cue-ball on the right

DIFFERENT TYPES OF CUE-BALL CONTROL

Cue-ball control is attained by imparting the different forms of spin generated by a player striking the cue-ball at varying points on its surface. In this respect you are best advised to think of the cue-ball surface as a clock face. Indeed, there is a practice cue-ball with a clock face painted on it on the market. It's a terrific idea, but even if you cannot get hold of one, it is easy enough to imagine the hour marks in position.

There are three main types of spin. They are topspin, backspin and sidespin.

TOPSPIN

Topspin is used unwittingly by beginners on most shots as it is the easiest type of spin to apply. If we use the clock-face idea, topspin is imparted when the cue strikes the cue-ball at twelve o'clock. This results in the cue-ball following through down the table. Remember, as you strike the ball progressively nearer its centre the less spin, and consequently follow-through, will be generated.

Topspin can only be achieved effectively by addressing the cue-ball well above centre. But never hit down on the white. And when striking the cue-ball at twelve o'clock always make sure that the bridge hand is raised sufficiently so that the cue is as parallel to the cloth as possible.

To impart topspin the cue-ball must be struck at twelve o'clock (below), while for backspin the ball should be hit at six o'clock (below right)

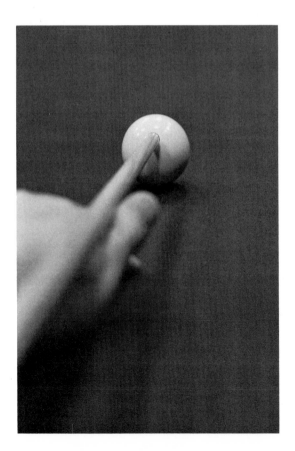

BACKSPIN

Striking the cue-ball below centre will cause backspin to be applied, it will either stop the cue-ball dead after it has made contact with the object-ball, or make it roll backwards. The precise effect depends on several variables – exactly where the player strikes the cue-ball, the distance between cue-ball and object-ball, the angle of contact – and so on.

The Stun Shot

If contact is made just below centre only a tiny amount of backspin will be achieved, and if it catches the object-ball squarely the cue-ball will stop. This is called a stun shot.

The Screw Shot

As one strikes further down the cue-ball towards six o'clock, it will shoot backwards away from the object-ball after contact. This is known as a screw shot, and is the one that beginners marvel at. It looks like magic when a top professional powers home a spectacular pot from long distance and screws the white back into perfect position, but this trick is an open secret which everyone with a modicum of application and determination can master.

We travel the length and breadth of the globe these days playing in tournaments and exhibitions, and the one question that never fails to crop up, from Bournemouth to Bangkok, is how to screw the cue-ball back. It is a fascination for every budding snooker player. Much of the skill is in feel and touch, but I will attempt to explain exactly what is necessary to complete a successful screw shot.

First of all, the preparation is important. To get the power into the shot it is advisable to make longer, smoother preliminary addresses than usual at the cue-ball before you hit it. Then let your cue do the work. Try to maintain the smoothest possible cue-action, pause at the end of the backswing, come through the ball at six o'clock and, perhaps the most important tip of all, follow through on a straight line. Your cue should be at maximum acceleration just as it goes through the ball. These are the essential ingredients. Now just think about a number of common mistakes made by players attempting a screw shot and see if they apply to you.

The waggles before the shot should not be short and jerky. This makes the shot more difficult as it causes a long final backswing and so a loss of rhythm. Rhythm can also go out of the window if, as some people think, one grips the cue more fiercely for shots that require power. This is a misconception. Backspin is directly related to timing and not strength. Therefore always attempt to keep body, and particularly shoulder movement down to an absolute minimum.

However, the most familiar problem coaches have to remedy occurs when players try to screw back by digging the cue-tip down into the bottom of the ball. Apart from the fact that this only generates an insignificant amount of spin, having the cue in the air leads naturally to a loss of accuracy, and there is no point in sacrificing the pot in order to attain position. It is accepted that the cue-ball has to be struck low down to achieve backspin. Therefore to avoid hitting down on the white just lower the hump of the bridge so that (as with the topspin shot) the cue is running as horizontally as possible to the bed of the table on contact.

Getting all this right and ironing out any faults is vital, because screw shots are an integral part of snooker. Joe Davis, the undefeated World Champion between 1926 and his retirement from the championship in 1947, once said that up to 80 per cent of the shots he used involved the application of some degree of backspin.

There is a simple and effective method of practising screw shots. Place the cue-ball on the brown spot and a red about 12 inches down the table. Don't worry about potting the red. Just try to screw the cue-ball back over the baulk line. Always make sure that there is ample chalk applied to the cue-tip as more miscues occur on screw shots than on any others. Once you've played that and mastered it move the red further down the table. Don't be frightened of the shot. You may miscue a few times but these are only the expected perils of learning. If you remember the basics – stillness of upper body, smoothness of cue-action, extended follow-through and lowering the bridge hand – you will soon make progress and start to pot the red ball.

But always remember that any exercise for backspin which has the cue-ball too close to the object-ball is futile. This is because, having struck the cue-ball·with backspin, the cue has to be withdrawn quickly otherwise you would be in danger of making an illegal second contact with the cue or your bridge hand. Also, if you are too close, you will not have time to complete a full follow-through, and because the follow-through is so vitally important for this shot the whole exercise will be rendered useless.

Stun and screw shots belong basically in the same group. They are defined as stun or screw depending on the relative position of the balls, the distance they are apart, where the cue-ball has to strike the object-ball, and also the strength of shot.

Because the cue-ball gradually loses spin the further it has to travel, a screw shot with the white and object-ball 12 inches apart would become a stun shot if the distance between them increased, for example, to 4 feet. This is because after travelling 12 inches there is ample spin remaining on the white to make it screw back. However, after 4 feet the majority of the original spin has dissipated, and it is as much as the cue-ball can do to stop at the point of impact. Arbitrary distances are used in this example to illustrate the point but the same principle applies for all shots in which the cue-ball is hit below centre.

By slightly varying where they hit the ball competent players can stun the white off the object-ball at any point of a wide arc. The advantage of this is obvious. By widening the angle at which the cue-ball leaves the object-ball after contact players can manoeuvre it into a great variety of positions, increasing their breakbuilding options.

The Stun Run Through Shot

Another form of stun shot is called the stun run through. This is employed mostly on straight or just off-straight shots, and involves the white momentarily checking as it strikes the object-ball before running through for a short distance. This allows the player to strike the cue-ball with power and still avoid a deep follow-through.

You may realise that the same result can be achieved more easily by striking the ball with topspin at slow speed, and it is quite reasonable to question why the stun run through shot, with its small margin for error, is used at all. But the answer is simple. Firstly, by hitting a ball crisply, a player is relying less on the table running 'true' than when dribbling the ball towards the pocket at snail's pace. This is similar to the golfer who decides to chip the ball towards the hole when just off the green as opposed to putting it. Secondly, most players find it considerably easier to maintain straightness in their cue delivery if they are pushing it through at reasonable speed. This stun run through shot allows them to do just that.

As with the ordinary stun shot it would be impossible for me to tell you the precise point on the surface of the cue-ball to strike to achieve this effect. Again, it all depends on the distance between cue-ball and object-ball. Obviously twelve and six o'clock must be avoided, but the 'sweet spot' for a particular shot like this can only be learnt by experiment and continued practice. The stun run through shot is one I play quite a lot and over the years it has helped me out of some difficult situations. Like all the other stun and screw shots, it is a vital part of the advanced player's 'armoury'.

SIDESPIN

It would not be going too far to say that no other single facet of snooker causes more bewilderment and frustration than the use of sidespin.

Even the top players only use 'side' (as it is known in the professional game) when it is absolutely necessary for position and when there is no viable alternative. Its application is so complicated that it almost always increases the risk of potting error. Having said that, do not be deterred. Side, used properly, can improve a player's positional and safety play out of all recognition. When players get to the stage where they can control their cue-action, and can deliver it in a straight line, then the time has arrived for them to begin dabbling with side and unlocking its mysteries. The use of side can be a source of great satisfaction. But remember that the ground rules for sidespin are use it only when necessary and always be aware of its pitfalls. Without a shadow of doubt it is the most difficult of the three main types of spin with which to be consistently accurate.

Before we go any further it may be helpful to explain the effects of side on one particular shot. If the cue-tip strikes the white on its right-hand side, at three o'clock, the ball is initially pushed to the left. But as the spin begins to take effect the ball will begin to curve back to the right. Bearing all this in mind try a small yet illuminating experiment.

Hitting the ball at nine o'clock imparts left-hand side (below), and conversely, hitting it at three o'clock achieves right-hand side (below right)

Place the black on its spot and the cue-ball approximately 12 inches away in a just off-straight line with the top pocket. Assess and play the pot by hitting the cue-ball without any form of spin whatsoever, ie plain, middle ball striking. Now, assess the potting angle again, but this time hit the cue-ball at nine o'clock, so that you are imparting left-hand side. The white is initially pushed out to the right, and if the shot has been played with some strength it

48

will make contact with the black before it has time to get back on line. It will therefore strike the black thinner than intended and the black will be overcut, hitting the near jaw. With right-hand side, at three o'clock, a similar shot will make a thicker contact sending the undercut black into the far jaw.

If these same two shots were played at a much slower pace, but with the same amount of side on the ball, what would happen? As the cue-ball would have ample time to come back on line it might even drift off line on the opposite side. So the shot with right-hand side could cause the black to be overcut this time and vice versa. Add in other factors such as the distance between cue-ball and object-ball, and the reaction of side when used alongside screw and topspin, and it becomes clear that the 'side' equation is always difficult and sometimes baffling to solve.

Only with constant and concentrated solo practice will you make much headway.

But after all the warnings about using side, it is still important to know how best to go about it. First, if you intend to use side, make sure you really do strike right or left of centre. The cue must still move on a straight line through the ball and must not move across it. If you place the cue-ball dead on the baulk line to apply right-hand side the cue must be to the right of the baulk line but still running parallel to it. And make sure you follow through. You often don't need to strike far off centre if your follow-through is good enough to apply the spin required.

The Swerve Shot

The most extreme shot which incorporates side is known as a swerve shot. For this the cue-butt is raised, and the ball is struck a downward blow. The most common mistake made by players attempting a swerve is aiming to strike the cue-ball well above centre. Instead the desired swerve is made more easily by striking below centre. The effect of the excessive spin on the ball causes it to take an arc. It is a stroke often used by an advanced player to escape from a snooker, but even the best player in the world can do little more with it than try to hit the object-ball. Unless the object-ball is hanging over a pocket the chances of potting it with a swerve shot are remote. Most players find they can swerve the cue-ball without too much problem. But the key to this shot is being able to control the degree of swerve.

The positive aspect of side is that it can be a very significant aid to positional play in that it alters the natural angle at which the cue-ball leaves the cushion. From a certain position on the table striking the cue-ball on one side will cause a widening of the angle it takes when it rebounds from the cushion. This is called 'running side' because the cue-ball travels further if it is applied. Conversely by striking the cue-ball on the opposite side the angle will be narrowed, and this is known as 'check side'.

(*Left*) *The swerve shot is a milder version of the massé. The cue does not need to be as vertical when hitting the white*

Initially in this case, the cue-ball shoots off to the left (below), before the right-hand side makes it swerve back to the right (below right). The arc of the cue-ball is much less severe than that in a massé shot

Side is also useful if you need to swerve to the right around an intervening ball. Hit just below the centre on the left-hand side so that the cue-ball initially swings out to the right around the obstacle, before the spin begins to work and drags the ball back to the left, and hopefully towards the ball you want to hit.

From experience of the many and varied hazards of side my best advice is to use it mostly when there is only a relatively short distance between cue-ball and object-ball. It is hard to calculate all the effects of side when the cue-ball has to travel a good distance before making its first contact with another ball. You can risk it sometimes if there is a ball hanging over a pocket and therefore the potting angle does not have to be precisely met. And it is also useful for a shot where getting the cue-ball back down the table to safety is more important than the pot.

Apart from the variables already mentioned an extra problem is that each table has its own idiosyncrasies, particularly the

The shot is mostly used as an advanced escape from snookers. The tremendous sidespin imparted allows the cue-ball to complete a wide arc in a small distance

heaviness, or thickness, of its cloth. This is called the 'nap'. As I've said, the cue-ball travels in a two way curve when side is applied, and this curve is directly affected by the nap. The heavier it is (such as in the first few weeks after a table has been recovered) the greater the effect of spin will be. The same cloth may also vary slightly from day to day according to the weather. This change may seem negligible, but in a game where fractions of an inch often make all the difference it could be vital.

Joe Davis said that to play a swerve shot you must raise both the butt of the cue and your bridge hand as downward striking from a height is essential. The palm of the bridge hand should be about 45 degrees to the table bed, and the hand itself should be resting firmly on the pads of the four fingers with the thumb cocked high. The blow to the cue-ball requires little or no follow-through, although one must feel the tip bite into the cue-ball as the stroke itself must be powerful. Not too hard or the ball will not have time to get back on line, but you will undoubtedly fail to achieve the swerve effect if you strike the cue-ball too softly to attain the necessary spin. Also bear in mind that the higher the butt is raised, the more spin and swerve will be attained. Some of the more elaborate swerve shots, known as massé shots, are played with cues at almost 180 degrees to the table, and they can make the cue-ball follow a semi-circular path in a very small area.

Hitting down vertically on the cue-ball creates the massé effect

PLAYING CONDITIONS

All full-size snooker tables are the same size. The spots for the colours are in exactly the same position on each, all the playing surfaces are green and the game is played indoors cosily tucked away from rain, wind and fog. But if you think that playing conditions are uniform on every table you would be wrong. Just listen to the stories from players in your local club side who have just returned from playing at a rival club where one or more of the tables were in poor condition. They will rant on in much the same way as a fisherman would exaggerate the size of his catch. Players often blame alien conditions for defeat and I can confirm that if you are accustomed to playing on a good table and have to play on a bad one it is extremely difficult to adapt. Problems can range from uneven slates, tight pockets, inconsistent reactions off the cushion, to the condition of the cloth itself. This is perhaps the most regular gripe.

Other complaints might be bald patches, beer stains, oily marks and even cigarette burns. These will alert you to what may be in store. However, you can also be caught out by a table, which at first glance looks fine, but which has a heavy nap and is therefore slow. On the other hand one which has virtually no nap at all can not only cause the speed to be too fast but might also make control difficult because the spin has nothing to 'bite' on. A player's natural game can be linked to the type of shot the table will allow. For example, deep screws or swerves may be impossible on a worn out cloth, while shots with topspin and side do not work as well on a heavy cloth.

At first all tables will look and feel the same to a novice, but as their shot repertoire widens they will begin to realise the subtleties of individual tables. The key to success, particularly in local amateur competition where conditions vary from the sublime to the ridiculous, is to know not only your own limitations but those of the table as well.

THE NAP

The nap on a snooker cloth is easiest to describe as like the pile on a velvet cushion; smooth one way, rough the other. The cloth has approximately 15 000 threads from the baulk end to the top, and each thread is made up of a mass of tiny fibres. All tables are uniform in that the nap runs from the baulk end (where the D is) to the top cushion. For this reason, a table is ironed in one direction only, always pushing the pile in the same direction. With the nap ironed in this way slow shots tend to run more truly, while playing against the nap, you cannot completely trust any cloth.

Clubs often have thick, durable cloths which, while not encouraging good snooker, are preferable only because they last longer. These cloths tend to cause the balls to run off a 'true course' and are particularly bad for shots when the cue-ball is a long way from the object-ball. Judging the allowance on a table like this is little more than guesswork.

The effects of the nap can be seen with one simple shot. Place the pink on its own spot, and the cue-ball directly behind it in line for the middle pocket. You would think that a straightforward pot rolling the pink into the pocket slowly should not pose too many problems. However, the nap of the cloth may cause the pink to set off in line for the pocket only to turn away just as it approaches and miss the pocket on the nearside. To get round this problem your aim should be at the far jaw of the pocket, or even slightly beyond, depending on the heaviness of the nap. When playing on a top quality cloth of the type used in professional events the aim must be at the middle of the pocket or just inside the far jaw because the object-ball will deviate little on a fine nap. But even so the nap effect is one that people who have both played and watched the game for years and years often do not fully understand.

There are also other hidden surprises with the nap. When hitting from the baulk end we know that the cue-ball will tend to drift to the right if you play towards the black spot using right-hand side. Left-hand side logically makes the same shot move to the left. But the situation is reversed when playing the cue-ball from the top cushion to the baulk end of the table, because the nap causes the cue-ball struck with right-hand side to drift to the left and vice versa. This is particularly useful to know when you are playing a safety shot off the pack of reds into baulk. With this knowledge you can curve the cue-ball to your advantage by hitting the cue-ball slowly.

Players often miss because they have forgotten about the nap. Always remember that the nap runs from the baulk end towards the black spot and top cushion. Without getting too scientific, the nap has a decided effect on the running of cue-ball and object-ball, particularly on slow and even medium paced shots. A fast shot, however, will discount any nap effect.

If you move your hand over the cloth you will feel the nap, up one way it is smooth, and down the other it is slightly rough and resistant. It is the same effect as on a putting green where a golf expert will tell you to hit the ball a little harder when putting 'against the grain'. My good friend Ian Woosnam, the Mighty Atom, tells stories of the 'grainy' greens in South Africa and Japan like I do about a particular 'heavy' cloth.

SUMMING UP

Cue-ball control is the secret of good, winning snooker. Don't expect to achieve it right away, or even in a matter of weeks. You must try shots out, practise and try them out again, even if you lose a few frames in the meantime. Look on it as an investment for the future and keep at it.

4 STRATEGY AND TACTICS

Players approach most games – whether it be football, tennis or snooker – with some sort of preconceived strategy. And though you should know your own strengths you should also try to become as aware as possible of your opponent's abilities and weaknesses. Obviously if you are playing a complete stranger this is not easy, but that does not stop you observing your opponent closely during the initial stages of the game. If they appear to be reckless and carefree some good safety play should produce plenty of openings. No one can pot everything. And even a cautious player will have to produce attacking play on occasions.

The aim of this chapter is to help you make up your mind correctly in what could be described as 50/50 situations. I will also try to explain how to place your opponent in the maximum trouble, and how best to extricate yourself from awkward and potentially dangerous positions.

BREAKING OFF

A good break-off shot is sometimes the most influential shot in a frame of snooker. The higher the level of the game being played the more importance is attached to the break-off shot. If I make a hash of it when playing someone like Steve Davis, Jimmy White or Stephen Hendry I may well be forced to sit in my chair for the rest of the frame watching them clear the table. That has happened to me on more than one occasion.

Some amateurs start the frame by rolling the cue-ball gently down the table into the reds. This is perfectly safe, of course, but it is all too easy for your opponent to glance the reds with their first shot and leave the cue-ball near the bottom cushion. By making a negative break-off shot, you hand the initiative on a plate to your opponent. There are many times I have looked back on a frame and realised that I had gained the upper hand as a direct result of a positive and accurate break-off shot. If you win the toss never entertain the thought of allowing your opponent to break. If you use the initial stroke to leave the balls safe and bring the cue-ball back into the 'sanctuary' of baulk your opponent will probably, without playing a stroke, be in some difficulty. How much will depend on the precise position of the balls.

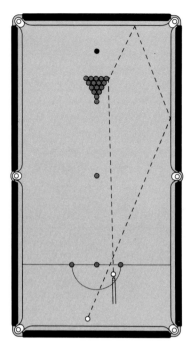
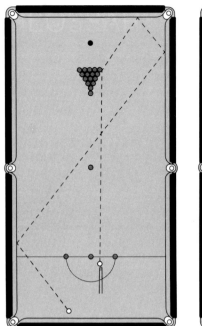
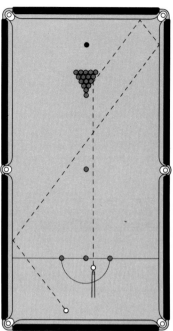

Figure 1 The beginners'
break-off

Figure 2 The professionals'
break-off – the cue-ball is
placed nearer the brown, and
'running side' (in this case
right-hand) is applied to the
cue-ball

Figure 3 An aggressive
break-off – hitting the third
red down with sidespin to
split the pack far and wide

Professionals may vary in their particular choice of break-off shot, but all are united in their use of side. Obviously a novice would be best advised to avoid, as we have seen, the intricacies of this type of break-off until they have experimented with this particular use of spin. *Figure 1* shows how side sends the cue-ball off the top and side cushions, inside the blue and into baulk when used to break off. The beginner will encounter fewer problems if they strike the cue-ball centrally, with no side, and aim for a quarter-ball contact on the outside red at the rear of the pack.

Figure 2 illustrates how the cue-ball will return to safety if it is placed on the right-hand of the D before being struck at break-off. The great advantage of this is that the ball will not swing in-off into the top pocket. Its drawback is that minimum displacement of reds occurs, and if your opponent commits a mistake there will be few potting options open to you. Therefore, as a player becomes more and more familiar with the use of side, it is best to think about the adoption of a more 'professional' break.

The break I favour in all my games is the one most commonly used by professionals. Assuming you are placing the cue-ball between the brown and yellow spots the idea (as in *figure 1*) is to apply ample right-hand side. This requires the cue-ball to be struck at roughly three or four o'clock. Other players prefer a much more attacking and so more risky break-off. This involves moving the white more towards the yellow on the baulk line prior to the shot. Even more side is applied, with the aim at the second red from the rear. The main object being to split the reds open as much as possible while still being able to return to baulk. Jimmy White can often be seen hitting the third red with bundles of sidespin (*figure 3*) in an effort to open up the game. This is a very positive break-off shot and one which can reap rich dividends, but only someone approaching Jimmy's ability should play it. If the shot is caught too thin it will kiss the next red down, career towards or even go in-off into the top pocket, and either way hand your opponent the possibility of an easy pot. Likewise, if the red is caught too thick there will be a similar outcome. Even if these dangers are avoided the next major obstacle is the blue on the way back to the baulk end. For an average club player using this break is likened to a high handicap golfer attempting to clear a 200-yard lake with a five iron. It's just not worth it.

You should, however, experiment with the different types of break-off shot. John Pulman, my colleague on the ITV commentary team and World Champion for twelve years during the 50s and 60s, says that he is baffled as to why all players, including the stars, don't often practise the break-off. Unlike any other shot, it is certain to be played every second frame. Get a good break-off and you can be the first to get points on the board, play a bad one and it's an uphill battle right away.

SAFETY PLAY

At an advanced level a player's tactical game is just as important as good potting and positional play. Safety play alone cannot win matches and at the top level you have to create chances with your tactics. It's no good relying on your opponent missing. However, at a lower level, a good potter can be beaten by a cunning exponent of the art of containment. You can see this in any local league. Sooner or later a young whizz kid, usually renowned for knocking them in from everywhere, is suddenly stopped in his tracks by a player with greater experience who consistently puts him in awkward positions, and then mops up the easy ones.

Safety is of less concern to the novice than to the advanced player. The beginner is probably playing against someone with insufficient skill to warrant defensive tactics, who even when presented with a perfect breakbuilding opportunity would probably not make a big score. Get beyond the novice stage, though, and it matters a lot.

Aside from the numerous occasions when there is no scoring stroke possible there are no set guidelines about whether or not to play safe. As I said earlier the responsibility for making this decision rests entirely on the shoulders of the player who will consider his or her own ability, confidence and the risks involved. Experience, or lack of it, will guide your judgement.

PLAYING THE PERCENTAGES

A whole range of factors should sway your thinking when it comes down to deciding whether to take on a risky pot or play safe instead. These include the score, both of the frame and the match, how many balls there are left on the table, the condition of the table itself and, crucially, the feeling a player has about the particular shot. Having made a series of sizeable breaks on the way to opening a significant lead a player may go for a difficult pot because they feel they are playing well. Twenty-four hours later the same player could have lost this confidence and should therefore elect to play safe. It is this ability to know your own limitations that can separate the good from the very good player.

Another important factor in the decision making process is the risk of a shot weighted against its reward. My good friend Rex Williams, a former World Billiards champion and still one of the most formidable safety players in the professional game, likens it to a business decision. He maintains that it is never worth taking a big risk for a small gain, unless forced into it. Likewise a big risk for a big gain can also lead to a player's downfall. The most attractive proposition is to take minimal risk for a big gain. That is as sensible a policy to follow in snooker as it is in business, an area, may I add, where Rex has also been successful.

Constantly leaving your opponent in a difficult position will not only undermine their morale, it will also make your being given a breakbuilding opportunity much more likely. As a frame develops most players become increasingly frustrated when not given the chance to pot balls, and this frustration leads to them attempting dangerous or even foolish pots. If you find yourself on the receiving end of safety play ... be patient.

SHOTS TO NOTHING

As I have said a small risk for a big gain should not be missed. Therefore, it always pays to be on the lookout for a 'shot to nothing' right from the start of a frame. These are best defined as shots with a chance to pot and only a negligible risk of leaving your opponent a chance if you miss.

In *figure 4* the quarter-ball pot can be attempted into the right-hand top pocket, with the player knowing that at the same time they are playing a safety shot. In this instance even if the red caught the jaws of the pocket, and stayed nearby, the player could count himself unlucky if one of the other reds and/or the green or blue did not block his opponent's path to it.

If the red is potted and the cue-ball finishes in the position shown in *figure 4* the green can be potted, without too much difficulty, into the middle pocket. If a good position is gained on the reds a sizeable break could be launched. Conversely if the cue-ball runs on to the baulk cushion, and in the process makes potting any of the baulk colours too risky, the alternative is to roll

Figure 4 The classic shot to nothing – pot the red into the top pocket and return to safety in baulk

Figure 5 A screw-back shot to nothing

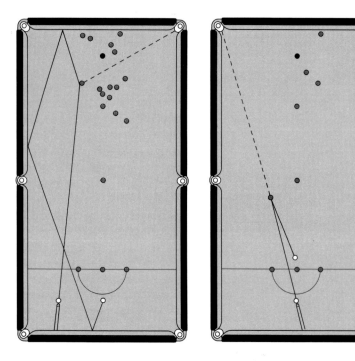

up behind the green or brown and snooker the other player.

Always bear in mind the possibility of playing a shot to nothing without using the cushions. For example, using a deep screw-back shot as in *figure 5.*

Sometimes players who recognise a shot to nothing fall down by not concentrating enough on the pot. They make half-hearted prods at these pots saying 'I knew I wouldn't leave much on if I missed'. This is very negative. Shots to nothing are a luxury and should be treated as such. Maximum concentration should be applied to the pot element of the shot. Otherwise you are denying yourself the chance either to initiate a break or place your opponent in trouble. You must ask yourself if you are trying to win or just trying to stop your opponent playing.

BE POSITIVE

Always bear in mind that there are two noticeably different forms of safety play, one is positive and the other negative. The most desirable in any position is to be positive or even aggressive and aim to place your opponent in a difficult situation. Try and force them to make mistakes. Negative safety merely prevents your opponent from having an easy shot, and even if you succeed your opponent may seize the opportunity to put you in trouble with their next shot. On this basis negative safety should be avoided unless there is absolutely no alternative way out of trouble.

If a frame is contested between two players of above average capability it is common for the early stages to be dominated by safety play. The cue-ball will make thin contact with the reds and be returned to the baulk area time after time. But if not enough thought is put into these strokes then a 'get it back into baulk and that will do' mentality might develop. Just going through the motions like this, however, means that players fail to give their opponents the maximum difficulty on the next shot. Always try to imagine the completed shot and where the cue-ball will end up. Snooker is very similar to golf in this respect. Your concentration on the game, and on the shot, must be clearly focused, and the position of the balls must be scrutinised so that you can weigh up the various options open to you as clearly as possible.

So spare a thought for the top players when you are sitting in your armchair at midnight in front of the television and waiting to see the conclusion of an important match. Don't curse them if they keep checking on the position of the balls before they play a shot. I have burned the midnight oil myself many times and the nearer to the end of a match the more important it is to choose the best shot open to you.

As we saw with the break-off shot, splitting the reds up far and wide will increase the odds on you making a big break, as long as your opponent lets you in. Therefore, if you can be sure that you will not leave a pot on with a safety shot, even after the break-off, it is sensible to move the reds about a bit. This will not only make it more difficult for your opponent to play safe, it will also add pressure with the knowledge that loose reds are available. When playing safe in the early stages of a frame knowledge of the angles that the cue-ball will come off the object-ball and the cushions is essential. Without it the path of the cue-ball back to safety can not be accurately assessed. And when there are a lot of balls on the table the path back to baulk is littered with obstacles. So balance your play, but always be positive.

ATTACK OR DEFENCE DILEMMA

Every snooker player faces the problem of striking the right balance between attack and defence. When to 'have a go', and when to play safety. And there are no stock answers to this dilemma. There are times for caution and bravery according to the circumstances, whether it is the position of the balls, the score or simply how you feel.

In *figure 6* the player has potted a red, and the cue-ball has finished in the baulk area. Should you trickle up behind the brown and leave your opponent in a snooker? Or do you pot the green and attempt to continue your break? In this instance, the key factor is the position of the reds. The green pot is a tricky shot and by no means a certainty. Therefore if the reds are well split and a missed pot could result in an easy pot for your opponent, the sensible shot is to roll up behind the brown. However, if the reds were clustered together and in a safe position

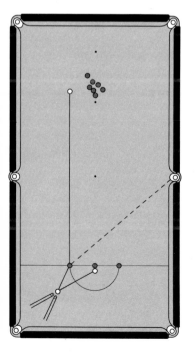

Figure 6 The attack or defence dilemma. Should you set a snooker by rolling gently up behind the brown, or pot the green into the middle pocket?

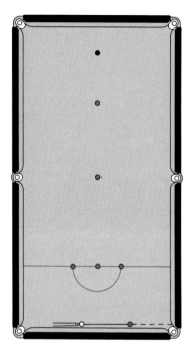

Figure 7 A straight pot is of no use if the black is required to win the frame

I would probably try to pot the brown, for two reasons. Firstly, four points should never be sniffed at, and if the pot was successful there would be no difficulty in returning to safety off the pack of reds with your next shot. Secondly, any reasonable player could get out of the snooker fairly easily by playing off the cushion and gently rolling into the pack of reds without disturbing them.

Of course, if the cue-ball was a little nearer the brown then the pot would become essential even if the reds were open. Potting the brown then would give a clearcut chance to win the frame rather than leaving the strong possibility of losing it. This is the kind of logical thought you need to apply before deciding on your attack or defence dilemma.

But individual judgments too, such as your own estimate of the chances of potting the brown in *figure 6*, must also be taken into account. Even at top level some players feel particularly confident of a certain type of pot or equally fearful of another.

Decisions also vary depending on the scoreboard. For example, in *figure 7* the pot on the last red is far from demanding, and will be taken on every time if a player leads by 34 points. However, if that same player is faced with that same shot when 34 points in arrears they will play safe as it is almost impossible to obtain any kind of position on the black which, along with all the six colours, is needed to snatch the frame by one point.

This is further illustrated in *figure 8* where a player 34 points behind, and desperate to knock the black into a pottable position,

Figure 8 Here are two safety shots from a similar position: playing the red into the black (which is on the cushion) and returning the cue-ball into baulk (left), or cannoning off the red into the black and at the same time returning the red into baulk (right)

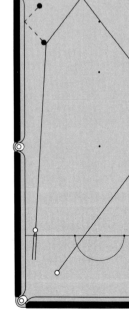

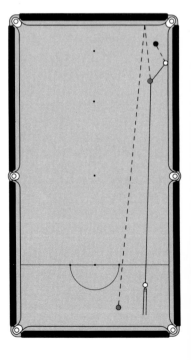

Figure 9 If it is impossible to gain a position on the reds after potting the blue, then just stun over and leave an easy return to baulk via the pack for your next shot (left). If you pot the blue and play safety at the same time you run the risk of leaving yourself a difficult next shot (right). Remember, a safety mistake could cost considerably more than five points

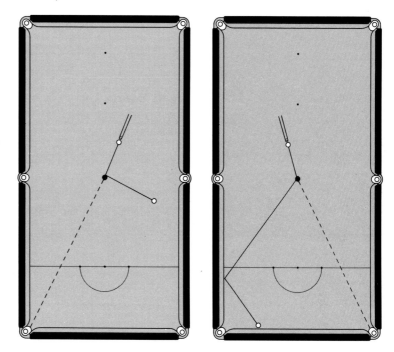

plays the red into the black (*figure 8 left*), and cannons the cue-ball into the black (*figure 8 right*). Both of these shots illustrate the kind of far-sightedness which make top class safety exchanges in snooker not unlike chess. If you are the player 34 points ahead in *figure 8*, with one red left, you should keep the black in its awkward position at all costs. Even a professional, who has a substantial but still beatable lead, will often knock one of the baulk colours under a cushion as an insurance policy against his opponent clearing the table in one go.

A common fault with novices is to play a pot-cum-safety shot on a colour, as in *figure 9*. Here the player attempts to pot the blue into the bottom pocket and take the cue-ball into baulk as an insurance against missing it. The logic of this shot has a major flaw, because even if the pot succeeds the player might be faced with a tough next shot playing safe off the reds. The five points scored for potting the blue pale into insignificance if it results in your opponent being set up with a good breakbuilding opportunity.

DOUBLE-KISS

A recurring difficulty in safety play is the threat of a 'double-kiss'. This occurs when the cue-ball and object-ball come together for a second contact, usually after the object-ball has struck a cushion. The problem with a double-kiss is that it usually stops the white returning to safety, and can even leave your opponent well placed. If, with experience, you know that there is a high risk of a double-kiss attached to a particular safety shot, try to find an alternative. If none exists, make the contact as thin as you can, and give the cue-ball a chance to get away from the object-ball before the object-ball comes back off the cushion.

SNOOKERING
Some players, very often old stagers, love nothing better than laying a snooker. They stand back, smile and say 'Get out of that one'. Fair enough. But never play a snooker just for the sake of it. There must always be a good reason. Remember that what follows from the snooker is usually more important than the snooker itself.

A cunningly conceived snooker may well turn a frame, or even a match, in your favour. This is definitely the case in *figure 10*. One player has potted the red, and although now able to pot the brown into the middle pocket is certainly unable to regain position on another red. However, electing to roll up behind the brown, instead of potting it, would leave his or her opponent in bundles of trouble. They might hit a red with no difficulty, but leaving the cue-ball in a safe position would require a great deal of luck.

This shot illustrates how a snooker can be used to full advantage. It leaves the snookered player with the almost impossible task of hitting the reds and not leaving some easy chances to pot. Many players only start thinking about snookers when they can't win without them. But you should always be awake to the possibility of snookers, throughout every frame you play. Of course, if you need snookers to win they should be your first priority, but remember that in this situation you are relying on your opponent forfeiting points, rather than scoring yourself. This is not very positive.

There are certain principles to stick to when playing for a snooker. Always try to leave the object-ball safe in case you are unsuccessful. Playing a snooker which sends the object-ball close to a pocket is very risky. If you need snookers on the colours it is generally true to say that your chances decrease along with the number of balls left on the table. But your opponent, if sensible, will try not to dribble the balls over the pockets. Because you can take advantage of the situation by potting the ball and at the same time manoeuvring the cue-ball into a position to lay a snooker with your next shot. Rolling balls over pockets is rarely the right policy, except when only pink and black remain.

It is also advisable, whenever practical, to play the cue-ball close behind the obstructing ball. This tends to make the escape harder. *Figure 11* shows the last four colours on the table. The player leaves the brown behind the black (*figure 11 right*) leaving a relatively easy escape off the top cushion with a touch of right-hand side. (*Figure 11 left*) on the other hand puts distance between cue-ball and object-ball and demands a more difficult escape using several cushions. If you need snookers to win, there

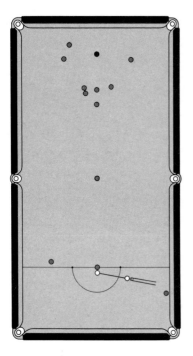

Figure 10 It is impossible to obtain position on the reds after potting the brown. Therefore it makes sense to leave your opponent in a snooker by rolling up behind it instead

Steve Davis *The modern maestro on his way to winning the 1989 World Professional title, his sixth of the 1980s'*

Tony Meo *Meo works things out during his victory in the 1989 British Open at Derby's Assembly Rooms*

Tony Drago *The Maltese Falcon, one of the most impetuous players on the circuit*

Neal Foulds *Using a cue extension to great effect at the 1987 World Championship*

Steve James *One of the game's most prodigious break-builders, breaks-off at the 1988 World Championship*

John Parrott *John in pensive mood overlooked by his lucky parrot mascot*

Alex Higgins *The game's bad boy considering his options with a worried expression*

Cliff Thorburn *Simultaneously pondering the situation and chalking the tip of his cue*

Jimmy White *The Whirlwind uses the table to his advantage at the 1988 UK Open*

Ray Reardon *His jutting out cue-arm, caused by an accident as a youngster, proved that unorthodox technique can work*

(Previous double page) The world's most famous snooker arena, Sheffield's Crucible Theatre during the seventeen-day marathon that is the World Championship

*Figure 11 This shows two
distinct ways of laying a
snooker from the same
position. The first shot (left)
is preferable to the second
(right) for two reasons. It is
easier to put the cue-ball
behind the black, and it also
leaves a tougher escape*

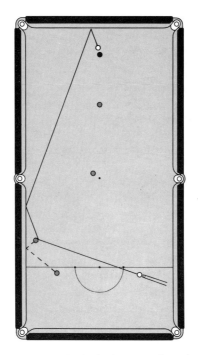
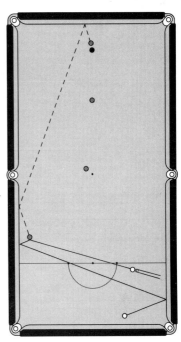

is little point in laying a series of snookers which require only the
simplest of shots to negotiate. But snookers can also be tactical
and even if they are easy to hit they can often be used to create
an opening.

With snookers, and with their escapes, a deep knowledge of the
table angles is priceless. That is why accomplished billiard players
often excel in this aspect of the snooker. After all the laying of a
snooker is very similar to achieving a cannon, one of the three-
ball-game's main scoring shots. Rex Williams comes to mind in
this connection, but I can also point out something Steve Davis
and I have in common, neither of us won the British Junior Snooker
Championship but we both won the same competition at billiards!

GETTING OUT OF SNOOKERS

As well as being able to lay snookers, you must also be able to
escape from them.

There may be the odd occasion when it is virtually impossible
to hit the ball 'on' from a snooker, but there is usually an escape
route by using one or more cushions or even a swerve shot. If the
cushions are used you need to calculate at what angle the cue-
ball will rebound. It can be useful to hit the white around the table
when you're practising, it will help you acquaint yourself with the
angles.

The single cushion escape should, in theory, be relatively easy,
especially if there is only a small distance between the cue-ball
and object-ball. Despite this, for ordinary players, the failure rate
on this type of shot is surprisingly high. Most players miss for two

Stephen Hendry *The young
pretender turned king of
snooker at the scene of his
triumph in the 1990 World
Championship*

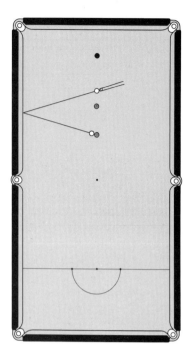

Figure 12 This shows the V-shape path of the cue-ball when hit correctly off a cushion

reasons. Firstly, because they are inadvertently applying side to the cue-ball. It is as important to strike the white correctly when attempting a snooker escape as it is when you are trying a pot. Secondly, players miss because they have assessed the angle – the point on the cushion that the cue-ball is required to hit – incorrectly. To find the correct angle for a one-cushion escape, examine the position of the balls, and aim for that point on the cushion which is equidistant between them. The path of the cue-ball will then follow a V-shape, as in *figure 12*.

On wide angles there is some variation from table to table. Professionals frequently play on tables whose cushions are newly covered, with high quality cloth. These cushions tend to 'slide' so that the cue-ball rebounds at a wider angle.

As you will find out if you are just taking up the game, many snookers require much more complex escapes, off two or more cushions. Only experience can give a player any insight into the correct way of hitting the object-ball in these especially tricky situations. However, as when laying snookers, certain principles apply to all players escaping from a snooker, regardless of their standard.

Never take an unconsidered swipe at the cue-ball, even though you may be content in the knowledge that you will hit the object-ball. Whenever you are in a snooker, try to plan ahead. Think what will happen to the object-ball if you do make contact with it. Will it knock 'safe' reds into pottable positions? Will it open up a 'safe' cluster for your opponent? If there is more than one escape route do not necessarily choose the one that makes contact with the object-ball most likely. Always work out the one that is the most advantageous in terms of safety, and go for that option. We have already said that a small number of penalty points during a frame are insignificant compared to the irreparable damage caused by hitting a snooker and leaving your opponent a straightforward breakbuilding opportunity.

Some readers will be wondering why players don't just miss the snooker on purpose, sacrifice the penalty points and concentrate on leaving the cue-ball in a safe position. Firstly, both the rules and the spirit of the game demand that a genuine attempt must be made to hit the ball on. Secondly, there is the 'miss' rule. If a referee does not think that a player has made a sufficiently good attempt to escape from a snooker, he has the power to call a 'miss'. He then asks the player who laid the snooker whether he is prepared to play his next shot from where the cue-ball has stopped, or whether he wants the cue-ball replaced in its original snookered position and the offender made to play the shot again. This is a fair rule in so far as it stops a player gaining an advantage with a foul stroke. Unfortunately, it has also caused controversy when players have felt hard done by as a result of inconsistent refereeing. When making judgments based on opinion, as in this

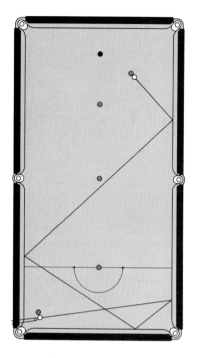

case, referees are bound to make the odd error, whether they are being too severe or more commonly too lenient with the player trying to escape from a snooker. Referees at professional level are more clued up about this rule than fellows refereeing the odd frame in a local league match, but even they can make mistakes. The 'miss' rule is a bit like the 'advantage' rule in soccer, it causes arguments but it is essential for the spirit of the game.

THE GREAT ESCAPE

The best escape I've ever seen is illustrated in *figure 13*. It was played by a young Devonian, Robert Marshall, at a critical point of his Pearl Assurance British Open quarter-final match against Welshman Steve Newbury in 1990. Marshall, trailing 3–4 in frames, led by 28 points in the eighth frame with just the colours remaining. With the cue-ball resting against the green there was no alternative but to apply a huge amount of right-hand side to the cue-ball and play off no less than four cushions. He did it, and it was only one of five successful snookers that Newbury laid at the conclusion of that frame. It was such an intricate and perfectly played escape, particularly considering the overall match situation, that in my television commentary I said, 'That's the best single shot I've ever seen.' Marshall hung on to win the frame, and then went on to win the match 5–4.

Figure 13 Marshall's great escape shows tremendous skill, self-confidence, and above all, a deep knowledge of the table's angles

SUMMING UP ON SAFETY

It is in safety play that the thinking snooker player has the edge over the raw potter. And watching a prolonged, high quality safety duel between two players can be as fascinating and absorbing as seeing a century break.

Always keep in mind the principles I have outlined, and try to digest the differing types of safety shot that you see so often on television.

Experience is a great teacher in this department, as much for deciding what to do as actually doing it. But youngsters shouldn't worry, the old adage 'You can't put an old head on young shoulders' doesn't always apply and I have seen many eighteen-year-olds who have learnt more in a few years than some players have in a lifetime. Just keep practising, watching and learning.

If a shot can be reached by stretching over the table there are certain instances where the placing of the back leg on the cushion rail can promote stability

5 DIFFICULT AND ADVANCED SHOTS

There comes a stage in almost every frame where a player has to take on a difficult shot. Even at the break-off your opponent may have left the cue-ball hard against the baulk cushion, and you not only have to hit a red but try to play safe at the same time. Or it may be at some stage that you find yourself snookered and have to swerve round an intervening ball in order to complete a successful escape. These are the kind of situations and shots required that I will concentrate on in this chapter.

AWKWARD BRIDGES
It will not take you too long to realise that the orthodox bridge is impossible to use for some shots, either because the cue-ball is close to a cushion or close to another ball. When it is out of your normal reach you will need to use one of the types of rests we discussed in chapter 1.

However, it is always difficult to be accurate with shots where the cue-ball is impeded, either by the cushion or by intervening balls. In these situations many players put themselves at an immediate disadvantage because they do not bridge correctly. Some contort themselves into shapes that an escapologist might use to extricate himself from a straight-jacket, and then stare in disbelief when the shot is missed. In positions where more than basic bridging is required bad habits must be cured right at the start. The longer a player adopts the wrong technical approach the harder the habit will be to break. And remember the first thing a player must do with any shot is to chalk the tip to decrease the possibility of a miscue.

BRIDGING FROM UNDER A CUSHION
If the cue-ball is tight under the cushion it is best to place all four fingers of the bridge-hand on the cushion rail, as flat as possible, so that the fingers can grip the surface of the cushion and thus keep the bridge solid. One can keep the fingers flat by dropping the wrist below the level of the cushion rail. Obviously there is only a limited area of the cue-ball to strike but, even so, do not be tempted to hit down on it with a bridge balanced on the tips of the fingers. This makes accurate sighting and clean striking extremely improbable.

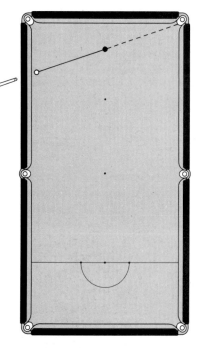

Figure 14 Practise straight blacks off the spot with the cue-ball tight under the side cushion

It is also important to realise your limitations with this kind of shot. Don't be over ambitious by trying to play a shot with lots of side or at speed. Always keep things as simple as possible. It is also helpful to shorten the length of the preliminary addresses to the cue-ball so that there is very little backswing. You will have more control on the shot in this way.

Let us assume that you are attempting to pot a straight black off its spot into the top pocket with the cue-ball tight under the cushion, as in *figure 14*. You will be looking down on the object-ball in this situation, and so the preliminary assessment of the potting angle, before you actually get down to play the shot, takes on more importance than usual. There is a tendency to look up to see how you have fared, but you must consciously try to keep all movement down to a minimum throughout the shot. And remember, shorten that cue delivery. One practice exercise designed to improve your cueing off the cushion is an extension of the test designed to examine your normal cueing. Instead of placing the cue-ball on the brown spot and playing it up and down the spots, take it back in a straight line to the baulk cushion and try the same shot from there. Also practise the black pot shown in *figure 14*. Don't expect a 100 per cent success rate with either because they are very difficult shots. But keep trying until you have some success, and you will feel more comfortable with the cushion-bridge.

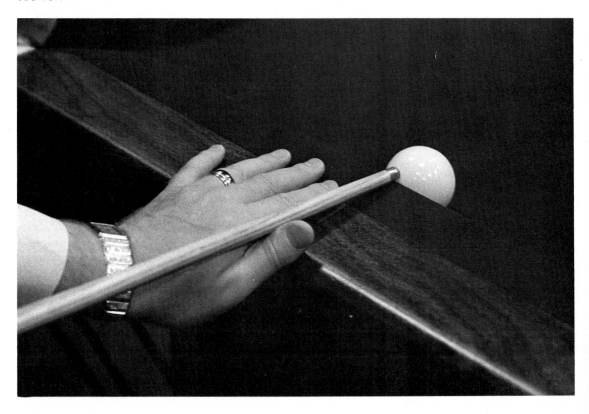

By placing four fingers of the bridge hand on the cushion rail a player is able to execute a shot from near the cushion with greater freedom

THE LOOP BRIDGE

Another type of bridge is needed when the cue-ball is a couple of inches out from the cushion, but still not far enough away from it to allow the normal bridge. This is called the loop bridge.

These shots are dreaded by players of all standards. Lower the wrist below the level of the cushion rail and consciously try to keep the cue-action as smooth as possible

This time the fingertips grip the green baize, with the heel of the hand resting on the wood. For this bridge, unlike any other, instead of cocking the thumb up you should keep it straight and move it under the forefinger until it touches the joint of the middle finger. Then loop the forefinger around the cue. The cue then uses the outside of the middle finger and the inside of the forefinger as its guiding channel. Some people never allow themselves to

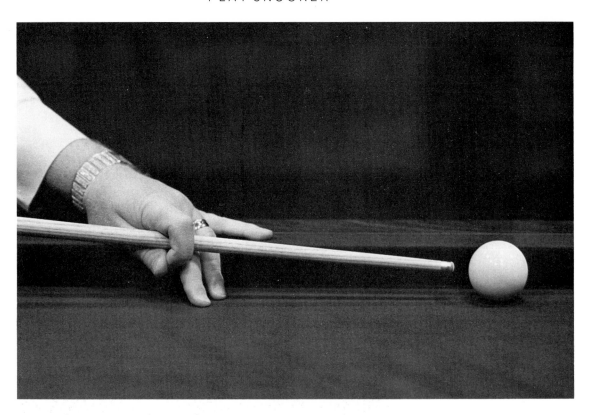

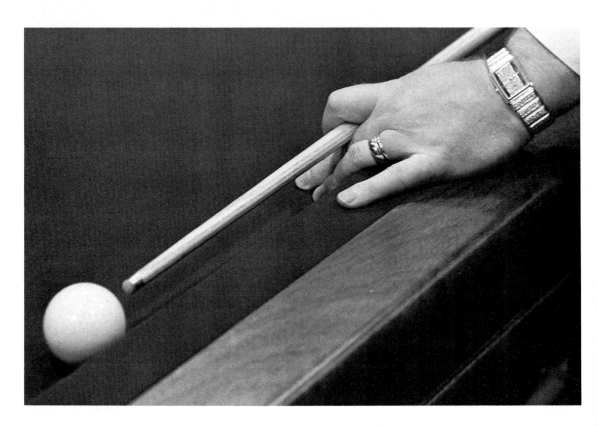

(Right) Notice how the little finger of my bridge hand is resting on the cushion to provide extra support and stability (top). The looped bridge is used quite often when the cue-ball is touching or in close proximity to the cushion (bottom)

trust this type of bridge, and therefore rarely use it. However, if you can control the cue this shot's great advantage over the conventional shot is that it allows you to play with power.

BRIDGING OVER INTERVENING BALLS
Some people would argue that a shot over an intervening ball is the hardest of all to master. However, while these shots undoubtedly present major headaches even to the top professionals it is important not to be frightened of them. With a sound technique and confidence in your own ability you can play them quite competently.

Without the stability that the two fingers give – at best this shot will go astray – at worst the cue will be so insecure that it will wobble, hit the object-ball and a foul shot will have been committed

To play this shot the heel of the hand must be raised off the bed of the table, so that your bridge is at least at 45 degrees, rather than horizontal, to the table. Rely particularly on your middle two fingers for stability. They should be slightly forward, with the other two fingers slightly back. It is all too easy for this bridge to wobble. So spread the fingers as widely as possible and apply enough pressure on them to gain a solid grip on the cloth. Always try to avoid an over-long bridge by placing your front fingers as near as possible to the intervening ball. But be careful not to cause a foul stroke by touching it, either with your fingers or the cue!

The height of the bridge should vary with the distance between the intervening ball and the cue-ball. The closer they are the higher the bridge. Sometimes, in an effort to get the cue coming down on the white at a steep enough angle to play the shot, you may have to raise the tips of the forefinger and little finger to ensure the necessary elevation in the bridge.

But above all, don't hurry the stroke or try anything too fancy. The cue-tip should strike into the ball and not stab at it. Take the time to find the correct position for your bridge. Be purposeful, develop the necessary technique, believe in its effectiveness and keep cool. These shots are tough but they are not unplayable.

PLAYING WITH THE REST

Sometimes, the cue-ball finishes in such a position that the rest has to be used for the next shot. There are times when I think that I am not the world's worst rest player, but I must be a close second. Over the years I have developed an ability to play left-handed and this has drastically cut down the number of times I have been forced to use the rest. My lack of confidence is shared by many, and even masters of the game like Joe Davis and John Spencer were strugglers with the rest even in their heyday.

Although the rest is a weakness of mine I know that if it is used correctly, and regularly, from the time someone takes up the game there should be no problem. Just look at Jimmy White, in my view the finest rest-player in snooker. The Whirlwind started playing when he was so short that he had to use the rest a lot.

I may not feel good when using the rest myself, but I do know the theory. And, just like Peter Alliss's advice in *Play Better Golf*, my advice is sound. Peter's numberplate, PUT 3, tells its own story about his troubles on the green.

When using the rest players often try to balance its head on the table, while holding the butt in the air. However, it is always best to anchor the rest firmly to the surface of the table with your free hand. Unless other balls intervene the rest head should be placed between 6 and 8 inches from the cue-ball, similar to your bridge-hand. Try to keep the rest still.

Novices tend to use the rest with its head 'tall way up', but unless you are required to put topspin on the cue-ball (by striking it high)

When you are bridging over an intervening ball always attempt to get the middle fingers of the bridge hand gripping the cloth

I am not a good rest player but many of my fellow professionals are. The key is confidence. Never worry about using the rest, don't stab at the cue-ball, keep your head down and above all, be positive

Here I am using the rest the 'wrong' way. Always use the shallow 'V' unless you are hampered or need to place topspin on the cue-ball

it is advisable to use the more shallow 'V'. This allows you to strike the cue-ball dead centre.

The grip on the cue for rest shots is radically different from the one employed for normal ones. The cue should be held as you would pick up a pen, with just the first two fingers on top of the cue, and with the thumb, which regulates the power of the shot, underneath. The grip-hand will be turned away so that its back is facing towards the player's chin.

The cue is best held just below eye level so that the length of the cue can be used as a direct sighting aid. Obviously the player will be side on to the cue-ball because the cue action is basically little more than a push with wrist and forearm. And throughout this movement the cue arm should remain horizontal. Movement of upper body and head should be avoided, and a smooth rhythm is desirable. As with a normal shot the preliminary addresses should be controlled and rhythmical, and not just a series of disjointed jerks.

The same cue action applies when using the more cumbersome half-butt and three quarter-butt rests. These implements are brought out when a player has to reach the cue-ball at the other end of the table. To everyone's great relief the invention of the cue extension has made these monsters almost redundant at top

(Right) The grip on the cue should be pen-like. The cue-arm has to be horizontal to the cue-ball

level. However, if you have no alternative but to use either never try too complicated a shot. Medium pace is advisable, because a player can invite trouble by using too much power or by being too delicate. Even with the ordinary rest always be wary of doing anything too fancy. Many people have floundered when trying to play deep screw shots with them.

Unlike a normal bridge, a rest does not allow a player to run his or her cue parallel to the table's surface. Consequently a downward blow has to be struck, and this increases the likelihood of a 'scoop' miscue considerably. So always chalk your cue, consider the shot and play it carefully.

The spider is without doubt the most frightening of all the types of rest, especially for the beginner. Like the normal rest it is vital that a player holds it firmly in position. Otherwise the intervening balls, those the spider is designed to bridge over, will very likely be fouled. If there are a lot of balls around, and you cannot find a place for the rest handle, you should hold it in the air as firmly and steadily as you can.

The back hand (left for right-handers) should be used to anchor the rest firmly to the bed of the table

Keep the shot simple. By trying to do too much you may inadvertently apply swerve and therefore miss even the most straightforward of pots.

(*Above*) *This is the extended spider, which allows a shot to be played even if a number of balls are obstructing the cue-ball*

(*Right*) *The nearer the cue-ball is to the obstructing ball the steeper the angle needed on the cue to play the shot*

(*Opposite*) *The spider is without doubt the most difficult implement to use well. Even the great players struggle*

THE DOUBLE

A double is a shot where the object-ball is potted having hit at least one cushion. These shots are complicated and require a knowledge of a table's angles, but someone with a good eye for a double can fashion a frame-winning opportunity from a seemingly 'safe' position. Doubles are, for the most part, attempted into the middle pockets, although on the odd occasion they can also be played into the corners.

Obviously the success rate of a player with this type of shot depends on their ability to assess all the angles required. Both for the cue-ball and for the object-ball. This only comes with experience. You also need to know that the angle of its rebound is slightly affected by the speed with which the object-ball hits the cushion. Always remember, when playing a double, that the harder one strikes the object-ball the straighter it will rebound off the cushion, as in *figure 15*. Only by trial and error will you begin to accumulate knowledge necessary to succeed with doubles.

The most common double is undoubtedly the one into the middle pocket when the object-ball is close to the opposite side-cushion, as in *figure 16*. Some professionals, myself included, have no hesitation in deliberately going for this shot if there is no viable alternative. Once I even tried a middle pocket double to win the World Championship! But it didn't come off that time, of course. Going into a middle pocket is relatively easy for the object-ball because the target is wide open. This is not true for the corner pockets and doubles into them are usually risky. However, when

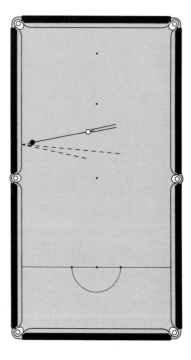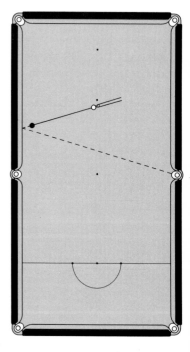

Figure 15 This illustrates how the object-ball can straighten off a cushion if an attempted double is played with too much pace

Figure 16 (right) The perfect double

Figure 17 The cross-double. This normally allows a player the luxury of a possible pot and a return to the sanctuary of the baulk

Figure 18 (right) A cocked-hat double

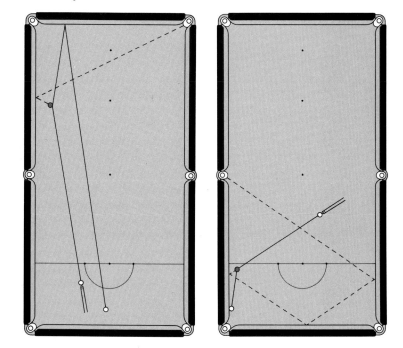

a corner pocket double can be attempted as a shot to nothing (see chapter 4), it can certainly be worth considering. In *figure 17* the player can clip off the red and get back to safety in baulk while the red could come off the side cushion and go into the opposite pocket. Obviously one must be totally sure that safety is certain before playing this shot. However, even then, it is tinged with danger as the red could catch the jaws of the pocket and stop in a simple potting position.

Figure 18 shows a position where a double into the bottom right-hand pocket could be considered, but even here it is better to attempt the 'cocked hat double', even though it's off three cushions. It would be a difficult pot, but, by leaving the cue-ball near the bottom cushion would give you a greater safety margin if you fail.

Be wary when playing doubles.

PLANTS AND SETS

A lot of confusion surrounds what the two terms plant and set actually mean. A set occurs when two object-balls, usually reds, are touching in such a way that a contact on the ball nearest the cue-ball will pot the further ball, providing, of course, that it has enough pace to reach the pocket. See *figure 19.*

A plant is a position where the two object-balls are not in direct contact. But the pot is completed by a player striking the nearest ball so that it strikes the furthest ball at the correct angle to send it into the pocket.

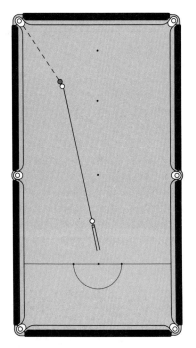

Figure 19 This shows two reds in a 'set' position

Sets can be missed if contact on the first ball is not full enough, but the margin for error is still wide. A player can, within reason, choose the angle needed to pot the object-ball, and still send the cue-ball into a good position. Indeed, it is sometimes harder to miss a set than pot it. They occur quite often and the astute player should always be on the look out for them. The secret of success with a set is not playing the stroke but actually spotting them in the first place. They look spectacular but are in fact quite simple.

However, plants are a totally different kettle of fish, and they require far more precise calculation. But if you have made your mind up to take on a plant, there is a tried and tested procedure to follow for the shot.

Using the example in *figure 20,* the first ball should be addressed as if it were the cue-ball. This tells the player where on the second ball that the first has to make contact. As a further sighting aid it is useful to aim at a point on the side cushion which is in a straight line to the point on the second ball that needs to be hit. If all this sounds complicated I have conveyed to you how difficult and problematical this type of shot can be. It is important to realise that the further the balls are from the pocket or the further they are apart the more likely it is that the shot will be missed.

These warnings are not designed to put you off plant shots, they are merely cautious pieces of advice. Great advantage can be gained from improving your understanding of plants, and this knowledge can act as an insurance policy against inadvertently potting the wrong ball, as in *figure 21.* Here, if playing safe off the

Figure 20 This shows a difficult plant, which involves striking the cue-ball into the first red so that it hits the second red and sends it into the pocket

Figure 21 (right) Always be on the lookout for a possible plant cum shot to nothing

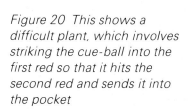

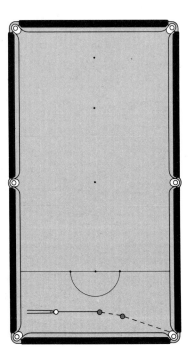

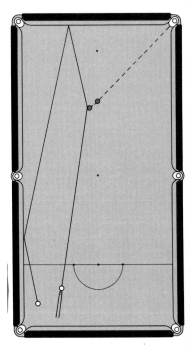

red, experience of the angles will help you avoid potting the pink and giving away points on a foul shot. But there are also more positive aspects to plant shots. Like doubles, they are particularly helpful when starting a break or even continuing a sizeable one.

Pool players, especially in America, play a whole range of plants as a matter of course. This is mainly because of the small table and the large size of the pockets. The first player to carry his pool expertise on plants into snooker was George Chenier, a Canadian, who on a visit to Britain in the fifties left the established professionals open mouthed with his range of what were then extraordinary plants. Of the modern day players my good friend Cliff Thorburn, along with his compatriot Bill Werbeniuk, are always very good with plants, both having long played pool for money over the length and breadth of Canada in their hustling days. But in the last few years all the top players have become very good in this department.

This shows a three-ball plant. The cue-ball strikes the red nearest the camera which strikes the middle red which in turn propels the furthest red towards the pocket

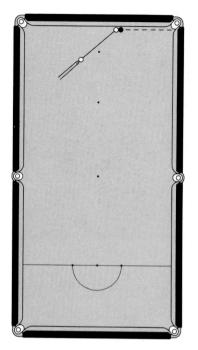

Figure 22 When potting along the cushion, always make sure that the cue-ball makes simultaneous contact with both the cushion and the object-ball

The plant or set is often not as complex a shot as it appears. The art is spotting them in the first place

POTTING ALONG THE CUSHION

One shot that many people find very difficult to master is the pot along the cushion. Players often hesitate before playing a shot like this even when the red is only a foot away from the pocket. And while getting the right angle on the object-ball is difficult don't be scared of trying it.

To pot the ball in *figure 22* the cue-ball must make contact with the cushion and the object-ball at exactly the same time. If the object-ball is struck before the cushion, or vice versa, the pot cannot be successful. Always remember that this type of shot is easier if you are at the top (black) end of the table. This is entirely down to the effects of the nap (see chapter 3) which tends to pull the ball into the top cushion. On the other hand, the nap will pull the ball away from the baulk cushion, thus making the pot more hazardous. If you are playing along the baulk cushion, you can offset the effect of the nap by hitting the object-ball with slightly more force than usual, so that it does not have time to drift off its intended course. But be careful here, too much pace can lead to the ball wobbling and thus bouncing out of the pocket. Hit accurately and at a sensible speed. If you are experiencing particular difficulty with this shot practise it on your own. By a process of trial and error you will not take long to discover where to aim and where you have been going wrong. In a match make your mind up on whether or not to risk the shot. If you take the bold course of action and attempt the pot there should be no half measures or tentative prods. Commit yourself and be positive.

DRAG

Backspin is most commonly used in screw shots, those which make the cue-ball recoil from the object-ball. However, it is also employed in the 'drag' shot, the main purpose of which is to allow the cue-ball to be struck firmly but slowly over a distance.

Say there is a red over a top pocket, the cue-ball is 9 inches away, and you want to stay in position to pot the black from its spot. If you just strike the cue-ball normally and roll it up the table, you are banking on the table running absolutely true and you striking the cue-ball dead centre. The intentional application of right- or left-hand side could cause even the easiest pot to be missed.

By striking below centre, as for a screw shot, you can apply a 'drag' effect. You can strike the cue-ball quite hard but because it is spinning backwards it 'drags' its way up the table. With good touch, you can control the amount of drag so that it runs out just before it reaches the object-ball. Before impact it will start to rotate forwards. Using drag can help a player be more confident and precise with positional play.

6 MIND OVER MATTER

'Practice makes perfect' is an old and overused adage. If there is something wrong with your basic techniques, you won't get very far, no matter how much you practise. And even if you were to lock yourself away as a recluse for ten years, with just a table and a set of balls to keep you company, you would still not emerge as an infallible genius who never missed a pot. Perfection in snooker is an impossible goal. But practice is essential for improvement, and that is what you should aim for.

It is simple to prove that any player, regardless of his standard, needs some kind of practice at regular intervals to maintain form. When I have returned from a fortnight's holiday in the summer the table seems as long as a cricket pitch. Shots that I usually pot automatically require more concentration, and I need practice to get rid of the ring rustiness and to polish up my strokes. Only then do I feel confident of acquitting myself well in a match against a fellow professional. And remember snooker is my profession. If this is what a relatively short lay-off does to a professional it is understandable that amateurs, who only play irregularly, become frustrated at their lack of accuracy. What else can they expect?

If you are sufficiently dedicated to practise on your own don't just set the balls up and go through the motions of playing a solo frame. You won't necessarily get the whole range of shots needed from this. Your precious practice time is best utilised if you break the game down into various components, and practise each one separately.

There are three basic reasons why players practise. Firstly, to combat a loss of form. Secondly, to prepare for a particularly important match or tournament, and thirdly, to improve their game. A novice's primary motivation would obviously be in the latter category, while a practice workaholic like Steve Davis puts in many hours for either one, or both of the first two reasons. If he is beaten in a big match Steve does not sulk or go home with his tail between his legs. Instead, next day, he will be back at the practice table finding out what went wrong. Steve is never satisfied. You would think that anyone whose game has been good enough to win the world title would stick to their technique. But Steve is always looking for a better way. Terry Griffiths too is a professional always looking to improve his technique.

Never be afraid to let anyone help you with the game

If you feel you have a nagging problem with your game practice is the way to solve it. Professionals are impatient to sort out flaws in their game and often revert to the basics in order to do so. And it always pays the beginner to go through a certain drill when practising. And it is practising the basics that counts.

First check your stance. Are your feet the right distance apart, is your body weight properly distributed and do you feel comfortable? Is there any movement of the upper-body or head when the stroke is being played? Is your cue action smooth and straight? Is your bridge solid and is it the right distance from the cue-ball? These are the fundamentals of the game. It may be boring to hear them mentioned constantly, but they are vital areas of technique. Imagine the mechanics of snooker as those of a car. Checking the basics every so often is the equivalent of a 10 000 mile service.

After a preliminary check-up of the basics devote some time to your weaknesses or bogey shots. Your bogey shots could be anything from potting a ball along the cushion to playing a screw shot. With practice my fear of using the rest has diminished. So whatever your problems may be, try to practise them until all the fear that previously surrounded the shot has been replaced by confidence. If this process is successful a weakness could become a strength.

Practice is important, but don't become a slave to it. I always maintain that, within reason, a player has to be in the right frame of mind to practise efficiently, and for a session to be productive total concentration is a must. It is always better to concentrate on your practice 100 per cent for an hour than 50 per cent over three hours. But don't misunderstand me. You will never be successful if you only feel in the mood for practice once a month. But there are times when too much is counterproductive. For example, if you practise three hours on the day of a match, will you have enough concentration for the match itself?

Two other major problems occur with solo practice. Firstly, there is always the danger of becoming too absorbed in the technique and theory of snooker. Solo practice does have a role to play but it is only possible to simulate the conditions you will find in a match by practising against an opponent as eager as you are to score and win. I once knew an amateur, who shall remain nameless, who used to spend hours gazing at his stance, cue-action and overall set-up in a full length mirror. I presume he wouldn't have done this in front of his practice partner. Needless to say this did not get him very far.

Secondly, constant practice can lead indirectly to a staleness, brought about by a dulling of the mental processes. A thoroughbred racehorse in spectacular form, often runs a stinker of a race towards the end of the summer, as the flat season reaches its conclusion; because it is over-trained. The same can apply to a snooker player. Steve Davis, a deep thinker about the game, in addition to being one of the all-time greats, realised the danger of over-involvement in a long season when the World Professional Billiards and Snooker Association tagged on the Hong Kong Open and Asian Open to the start of the 1989/90 campaign. Consequently, and at great risk to his number one position in the world rankings, he did not enter these two August tournaments. And his decision looked shrewd enough when he won the BCE International and Rothmans Grand Prix titles at the start of the British season. The mind will only take so much snooker because of the concentration required at every level.

Remember, practice won't 'make perfect', but done regularly and sensibly it will lead to great improvement.

PRACTICE EXERCISES

If we take it for granted that the most important basic of snooker is straight-cueing it is advisable to practise skill tests which highlight it. In chapter 1 we saw how cueing across the baulk line, without the presence of a cue-ball, can detect any deviation from a straight cue delivery. A double check to ensure accuracy is to play a series of straight pots into the top corner pocket, with the cue-ball at varying distances from the object-ball. Here no angle has to be assessed, but a full-ball contact is needed every time for a successful pot. Therefore regular misses can only arise from the loss of straightness in the cue-action, or from a defect in sighting.

Without doubt the most popular and useful solo exercise is known as the 'line up'. Place the six colours on their normal spots then put the reds in a straight line between them approximately 2 or 3 inches apart. The idea of this exercise is simple. Just try to compile a break using the normal red-colour-red sequence, but only making contact with the ball you are attempting to pot. If you are an advanced player try the same exercise but avoid hitting the cushion with the cue-ball during any pot.

An exercise of great relevance to a match situation is the black spot exercise shown in *figure 14*. Remember that most sizeable breaks are constructed around the black, and the aim here is to sink eight reds with eight blacks. By doing so you will get to know where to strike the cue-ball in order to make it follow the required path after a pot. There is only a small margin of error on a stun shot at the black to avoid being under the side cushion for the next shot. On the reds too a stun shot has to be delicately played. And it is also a good idea to practise splitting the pack of reds after potting either the black or blue from their spots.

I am sure that if you are prepared to practise enough you will begin to develop your own ideas and exercises. Whatever you do, try to make the most of the time you have available.

The aim is to pot reds and colours as during an ordinary break. It looks easy but after a few attempts you will discover it is not

THE MENTAL APPROACH

As in all aspects of snooker, players must find the right balance in their mental approach to the game. A player who accepts a mediocre performance with a shrug of the shoulders will never make a champion. Nor will someone who explodes with self-criticism at a bad shot. The key, I believe, is to get sufficiently annoyed if things are going badly to give yourself a pep-talk, but without losing your composure. This should act as a spur to make yourself do better and play harder, without lessening your concentration. I have even seen a few hotheads break cues in fits of pique after losing a match or even after missing an easy pot. This will get you nowhere, and shows a lack of self-control which you will need to cope with the ups and downs of this sport.

A good mental approach to the game is as important as a good playing technique. A player with an exemplary cue-action will never make the grade if his temperament is suspect, and similarly someone with limited ability can be very hard to beat if they are mentally strong.

One of the biggest mistakes an inexperienced player can make in a match is to take an excessive amount of time pondering each shot selection. Apart from being painful to watch and play against, this handicaps a player's fluency and rhythm. Granted, certain shots need longer consideration than others, but if, for example, you are in amongst the balls it is stupid to take two minutes over every pot. Bear in mind that the longer you take over a shot the harder it becomes to hold your concentration. The competent player gets down and plays the straightforward shots on something akin to auto-pilot. You can be brisk and businesslike without rushing on these, and take extra care on the more difficult shots.

There is a certain drill that should be followed on virtually every shot. You should always make your shot selection before you get down to play it. You must not change your mind in mid-stroke, this will lead to mistakes. You will hit the cue-ball in the wrong place, with the wrong spin or at the wrong speed. However, if you do change your mind, then stand back, alter your stance and start again.

Treat each shot on its merits. If you need a simple black off its spot to win the frame, play the shot as you would in practice. Don't take twenty cue-ups, or any extra time for the shot. I should know all about this. When I won the World Championship in 1985 I beat Steve Davis 18–17 on the final black. Considering that the tension was at fever pitch, and that the shot was the single most important one of my entire life, it would have been easy to take too long over it. Maybe I took a shade longer than usual getting down over the cue-ball, and even though my heart was pounding and my stomach churning, I played it in much the same way as any other shot, on its merits.

Even when you're leaning over the table to play an awkwardly placed shot always keep one foot on the floor. If a shot is played with neither foot in contact with the floor it is a foul shot

Always make sure that you are steady and comfortable before you play a shot.

In common with other sportsmen many snooker players allow a bad, expensive shot to linger in their thoughts to the detriment of their concentration. Thoughts of a missed pot or a poor break up of the reds are common in the mind of a losing player. I know it is difficult but always try to think logically. However much you re-play that shot in your head you have still missed it. Forget it and get on with the rest of the match.

Finally, it always pays to play the balls and not your opponent. Don't worry about the reputation of your adversary, you may become over-cautious and frightened to play your shots if you do. On the other hand, if you are over-confident and believe yourself to be superior to your opponent then you may take liberties. You might be tempted to take on risky pots and give the game away. Both of these attitudes, particularly the latter, are self-destructive. If you fancy a pot, and feel confident about your chances of success – go for it – regardless of whether you're playing a beginner or a champion. Never be intimidated by people's reputations. Respect them, but when you are at the table concentrate on playing to your own best standard. You've nothing to lose. After all if you're playing someone a lot better than you, and they play to form, they'll beat you anyway. So what? Concentrate on not beating yourself.

COPING WITH TENSION

Nerves, butterflies, tension, call it what you will, have afflicted every player at some point in their snooker 'career'. They can cause both mental and technical aberrations and may render a player helpless in a tense situation. Countless times I have seen good practice players struggling to put together useful breaks from good positions in competitive matches.

Nerves can cause the cue-arm to tighten up, and lead to what is called a snatch. A tight arm prevents the backswing from flowing and does not allow a pause before the cue comes forward. The much sought after, and practised, art of keeping yourself still gives way to an involuntary jerk which, more often than not, leads to the shot going astray. A free flowing cue-action tends to be less affected by tension in the cue-arm than a short jabby one. Relatively long preliminary addresses at the cue-ball can help to release tension. Try to discipline yourself to remain relaxed in pressure situations. Dene O'Kane has even resorted to pre-match meditation in a bid to relieve himself of tension in long matches. Maybe you won't have to go that far, but always remember that a relaxed player has a considerable advantage over someone bedevilled with nerves.

It is also common, when under pressure, to grip the cue more fiercely than normal. Feel your grip, and if it's too tight then loosen it up; it will help reduce the likelihood of a snatch. The year I won the World Championship, I held the cue looser than ever. I just felt comfortable in doing so.

Most players fall victim to nerves because their desire to win is overtaken by the fear of losing and the despondency associated with it. But it's only a game, and you should play it for enjoyment. Learn to enjoy the close frames as much as the runaways, and if you suffer from nerves consciously try to conquer them. If you succeed it is a satisfying feeling.

PRACTICAL STEPS WHEN PLAYING A MATCH

From the humblest club handicap, through national amateur competitions to the World Championship itself, there are certain dos and don'ts regarding preparation before playing a match.

Always leave plenty of time to get to the venue. Get yourself acclimatised to the surroundings, never rush or dash about beforehand. When Tony Jacklin played in the US Open in 1970, his friend Tom Weiskopf left a message in his locker which simply read 'Tempo'. He won by seven strokes. The same reminder would be useful to the snooker player. Preparing for a match at an unhurried pace, fosters composure and mental alertness.

Never wolf down a filling meal just before playing. Apart from the awful feeling you get when leaning over the table with a full stomach, excessive, ill-timed food consumption dulls the senses when they need to be at their sharpest. The same applies with alcohol. My advice is to avoid it, even in moderation. Some players drink quite large amounts during matches, and while it may soothe their nerves in the short term, I am convinced that in the long term alcohol's effects on a player's game are not beneficial.

Finally, I was told at an early age that if you look good, you feel good, no matter what you're doing, and I believe this applies in snooker. Obviously all professionals are reasonably smart as their uniform is a dress suit. In the amateur ranks, however, if two players are of equal ability and one walks out wearing a shirt and tie, neatly pressed trousers and polished shoes they will have an immediate psychological advantage over an opponent in denims and a tatty shirt.

Snooker is not an easy game, but don't make hard work of it. Even if you can't master some of the advanced shots I've described it does not mean that you cannot play a competitive game. And at whatever level you play, enjoy it. Professionals cannot function properly if they lose their love of the game, and they sometimes do with personal worries or staleness. Amateurs are not any different. Be keen, be nervous, play to win but if you let the game get out of proportion you will only increase the pressure on you, and let yourself down.

7 FINAL THOUGHT: WEARING SPECTACLES

Without good eyesight, or visual aids that help correct poor eyesight, the playing of good, accurate snooker is nigh on impossible. Indeed, for many years it was a widely accepted fact that without being a regular hawkeye it was highly unlikely that a player could become top class. This was first disproved by Fred Davis and John Pulman, before modern-day professionals such as Joe Johnson, Steve Newbury and myself also punched holes in the theory.

I have worn glasses for reading and everyday pursuits for as long as I can remember, but I was never able to wear them with any comfort while playing snooker. It was the age old problem for me because the rims of my glasses obstructed the line of sight on the shot. In 1979 my oculist recommended contact lenses. I adapted to them straight away, and that year I reached the final of the World Championship with victories over Steve Davis, Ray Reardon and John Virgo. And they were fine for a time. But long hours of travelling, and the constant putting in and taking out of the lenses were not good for my eyes. So in 1981 I decided to try a pair of swivel lens glasses that had transformed myopic Fred Davis from a short-sighted also-ran into a world-beater once again.

It was an important career decision so I was determined to go about it properly. I went to stay with Jack Karnehm for a couple of days. Jack, an accomplished billiards and snooker player perhaps best known as a BBC television commentator, had been trained by his father to make spectacle frames, and therefore he seemed to me to be the ideal person to consult. We spent the majority of my visit in Jack's workshop perfecting the design, until finally we felt the finished product was good enough to be tested on the professional circuit.

I must be honest and admit that there were times I felt like ripping them off and throwing them in the dustbin for good. It took me all of twelve, highly frustrating, and relatively unsuccessful months to get used to them, but once I had, my judgment of long shots improved 100 per cent. Long range pots, which previously had resembled balls of wool, suddenly became crystal clear and I began sighting pots like I had done when I was a teenager back home in Northern Ireland. As we all know I went on to capture my first major title at the 1984 Rothmans Grand Prix, and six months later, in April 1985, I beat Steve Davis 18–17 on the final black to realise my dream of becoming World Professional Champion. For days afterwards it seemed to me that the sports pages of the tabloid newspapers carried caricatures of me, invariably with the most huge pair of spectacles sitting on the end of a disproportionate nose. I did not mind for I knew that without the help of the glasses I would not have been celebrating the greatest moment of my life.

Not all players who feel their eyesight is defective, and take the appropriate corrective measures, will enjoy a new lease of life. However, if anyone – regardless of whether they are novices or advanced players – feels that their inability to sight the shot is inhibiting their snooker I would strongly advise them to seek ocular guidance.

In theory, the short-sightedness that affects many players can be remedied by the type of lens that sharpens up the blurred objects in the distance without affecting the near vision required for close-range shots. That is why lenses for snooker have to be bi-focal. Consequently a player cannot get away with using ordinary reading glasses because these will only sharpen up objects at a short distance.

Buying a pair of these specially adapted glasses can be quite expensive and of only minimal help to people with minor sighting difficulties. As I have already said they can also be a tremendous handicap at first. The glare from the balls can be alarming to the extent that one feels totally incapable of giving one's best. These are problems that any player would want to avoid if possible.

However, if a player's eyesight is so poor that long range sighting is little more than guesswork he has no option but to convert to glasses or contact lenses. If he does not only a miracle will stop his standard of play declining drastically. Spectacles breathed life back into my ailing career, I am sure they can do wonders for your game too if your eyes are not as effective as they once were.

By listening to a good player or a knowledgeable coach a player's standard can rise dramatically

SNOOKER:
TEN BASIC RULES

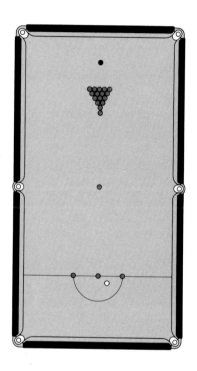

1. Snooker is played with 22 balls which are positioned at the start of the frame (or game) as shown here.

2. The cue-ball, which is used alternately by both players, can be placed anywhere in the 'D' for the first stroke but must thereafter be played from where it comes to rest except after an in-off or being forced off the table, in which cases the next player must again play from the 'D'.

3. Points are scored by potting and penalties. Each player must first attempt to strike a red (value 1). When he pots a red he must then play at a colour, the values of which are: black (7), pink (6), blue (5), brown (4), green (3), yellow (2).

4. The player should nominate the colour he is attempting, although the letter of this rule is not enforced in cases where this is obvious.

5. If a colour is potted it is replaced on its own spot and another red is then attempted and so on until all the reds have been potted.

6. The colours are then taken in ascending order of value until only the cue-ball remains on the table.

If at the end of a frame the scores are level, the black is replaced on its spot and the player winning the toss of a coin has the choice of whether he or his opponent takes first shot at it from anywhere within the 'D'.

7. Failure to strike a red involves a penalty of four points (the minimum penalty for any foul) but the penalty is increased to 5, 6 or 7 if, instead of a red, the cue-ball strikes blue, pink or black. An in-off is a foul carrying a penalty of four points or more if the ball which the cue-ball strikes before entering a pocket is of higher value.

8. Failure to strike a nominated colour also carries a four point penalty, or more if the ball involved is of high value. If, for example, green is nominated but pink is struck, the penalty is 6. If pink is nominated and green is struck the penalty is also 6.

9. Penalties often result not from incompetence or chance but from snookers. A snooker occurs when the balls are so placed that a player cannot strike the ball he is due to play without first hitting a cushion or making the cue-ball swerve.

10. If a player is snookered on the reds after a foul shot by his opponent he may nominate any coloured ball as a red. This is known as a free ball. If he pots it he scores one and can then nominate a colour in the usual way.

If no red remains, a free ball is valued at a number of points equal to that of the lowest value colour remaining and the colours are then taken in sequence.

For the purpose of this rule, a player is deemed to be snookered if he cannot directly hit both extremities of the object-ball he is due to play.

FOUL SHOTS

a] a player's cue-tip strikes the cue-ball more than once in the same stroke

b] if a ball is forced off the table

c] if a player plays with both feet off the floor

d] if a player plays before all the balls have come to rest

e] if a player strikes or touches a ball other than with the tip of the cue

f] by causing the cue-ball to jump over any other ball

g] by playing with the balls wrongly spotted.

After any foul shot, whether he is entitled to a free ball or not, a player can ask his opponent to play again.

GLOSSARY

Angled A player is said to be angled if the ball on cannot be struck directly because the cue-ball is so near a pocket that its path is obstructed by its jaws. (*Also known as 'knuckled'.*)

Baulk The rectangular area of the table between the baulk line and the bottom cushion.

Break A break is both an unbroken series of pots and the number of points scored by them.

Break-off The first shot of a frame, when a player has to strike the cue-ball out of the D into the pyramid of reds.

Clearance A player makes a clearance by making a break in which they pot all the balls left on the table, except the cue-ball.

Cue A wooden implement, usually made of ash or maple, used to play snooker.

Cue-ball The white, and the only ball in snooker that can be struck by the cue legitimately.

Cue-ball control This is acquired by manoeuvring the cue-ball using different weights and spins on the shot. Its main purpose is to make your next shot as easy or your opponent's as difficult as possible.

D The area of the table inside the semi-circle which protrudes from the baulk line.

Double A shot in which the object-ball is potted after it has made contact with one or more cushions.

Drag Backspin used to reduce the speed of the cue-ball as it travels towards the object-ball.

Extension This is a recent innovation. It is a tubular device which can be attached to the butt-end of the cue to lengthen it for awkward shots. Shots that once required the use of the more cumbersome half or three quarter-butt rest can now be played with one's own cue and therefore one's own cue-tip. However, even rests have extensions if required.

Foul shot An illegal stroke, which leads to a varying number of points being added to your opponent's score depending on the offence committed.

Frame A single game of snooker. A match consists of a prearranged number of frames. The name derives from the triangular frame which is universally used to set up the pyramid of reds at the beginning of a game.

Free ball	This is awarded if one player commits a foul shot and fails to leave a ball open for his or her opponent, that is to say open to be hit on either side with a direct shot. It prevents any advantage being gained in playing a foul shot deliberately. If awarded a free ball you can treat all the balls on the table as reds, and earn one point from a pot. If you nominate a colour ball it will be replaced on its spot, and you will go for another colour as usual. If there are no reds left on the table the free ball potted will count as the lowest value ball remaining. The ball will be respotted, and you will play the colours in their normal sequence. Remember, you cannot lay a snooker behind a free ball, unless only the pink and black remain on the table.
Full ball contact	This occurs when the cue-ball covers the object-ball at the moment of contact. This is the contact needed for a straight pot to be successful.
In hand	A player has the cue-ball in hand if his or her opponent has either knocked it off the table, or gone in-off with the previous stroke. The cue-ball is placed inside the 'D' for game to be restarted.
In-off	This is a foul shot in snooker, and a scoring shot in billiards. The cue-ball has gone in-off if it is pocketed after making contact with the object-ball.
Jump shot	This is when the cue-ball leaves the bed of the table and jumps over another ball, usually the object-ball. It is a foul shot.
Kick	The term given to a shot in which there is a bad contact between cue-ball and object-ball. It can be caused by a speck of dirt on the table or even chalk on the cue-ball. A kick will cause either or both balls to leave their intended course. If you get a kick the best advice is to have the cue-ball cleaned before your next shot.
Maximum break	If you pot 15 reds, 15 blacks, and all the colours in an unbroken sequence you will earn the maximum break of 147 points.
Miscue	A shot in which the cue-ball is not struck cleanly with the cue-tip. It usually occurs when a player is trying to apply sidespin or screw with power. Remember miscues are more common with chalkless cue-tips.
Miss	A miss is called by the referee who thinks that a player has not made a sufficiently good attempt to hit the ball on. If one is called the culprit's opponent can play the cue-ball from where it has come to rest or can ask the referee to replace the ball in its original position. The player who played the miss then has to try again. This rule is to prevent players sacrificing penalty points in order to leave the cue-ball in a safe position. The referee has to consider the standard of the player involved, because a two-cushion escape is relatively easy for a professional while it is a tall order for a novice with six months' experience.
Nap	The surface of the cloth, which is smooth to the touch running from the baulk end of the table to the top, and rough running from the top cushion to baulk. The nap affects shots played with

side, particularly those played slowly.

Object-ball   The ball with which the cue-ball is intended to make first contact with.

Pack   The name given to the cluster of reds. They are also referred to as the bunch.

Plant   A plant is a pot which involves a minimum of three balls. The cue-ball makes contact with the object-ball which in turn hits another ball into the pocket. Any number of balls can be involved in a plant. They can be complex and even dangerous to play.

Pot   A pot is completed by striking the cue-ball into the object-ball so that the object-ball enters a pocket.

Push stroke   This occurs when the cue-ball, cue-tip and the object-ball are in simultaneous contact. It is a foul shot. It usually occurs when the cue-ball and the object-ball are close together. Referees often notice a push shot because of the peculiar sound it makes.

Rest   Implements used to play shots in awkward positions, when the normal hand-bridge and stance are not possible. There are several types of rests, some more awkward to use than others.

Safety stroke   This is usually played to leave one's opponent in an awkward position. Its aim is not to score, but to force a mistake and gain a breakbuilding opportunity.

Screw   The name given to backspin applied to the cue-ball by striking it below centre.

Set   This is when two balls are touching, so that if the cue-ball strikes them at almost any angle the second ball will be potted.

Shot to nothing   This is where a player can attempt a pot safe in the knowledge that if they miss it is virtually guaranteed that the cue-ball will end up in a safe position.

Side   This is sidespin applied to the cue-ball by striking it either to the right or left of centre. It is used to aid positional or safety play.

Snooker   A player is said to be snookered if he or she cannot strike the object-ball directly, because its path is obstructed by one or more intervening balls.

Spider   A rest which gives the player the extra elevation needed for the bridge because intervening balls prevent use of the normal hand-bridge.

Stun   A shot which stops the cue-ball dead after contact with the object-ball using backspin. It is achieved by striking the cue-ball below centre. The actual contact point on the object-ball depends on the pace of the shot and the distance between the cue-ball and the object-ball.

Swerve   This is when an acute amount of sidespin is applied to the cue-ball to make its path curve. A player must strike down on the ball to achieve swerve. It is usually applied when escaping from a snooker without the use of cushions.

INDEX